SECRETS
of
INTERCESSION
AND
PRAYER

SECRETS

of

INTERCESSION AND PRAYER

A FOUR-MONTH DEVOTIONAL

Andrew Murray

CLC
PUBLICATIONS
Fort Washington, PA 19034

Secrets of Intercession and Prayer
Published by CLC Publications

U.S.A.
P.O. Box 1449, Fort Washington, PA 19034

UNITED KINGDOM
CLC International (UK)
Unit 5, Glendale Avenue, Sandycroft, Flintshire, CH5 2QP

ISBN (trade paper): 978-0-87508-765-8
ISBN (e-book): 978-1-61958-061-9

Unless otherwise noted, all Scripture quotations are from the Holy Bible, New King James Version, copyright © 1979, 1980, 1982 by Thomas Nelson, Inc. Used by permission. All rights reserved.

Scripture quotations marked RV are from the Holy Bible, Revised Version, 1881.

Italics in Scripture quotations are the emphasis of the author.

CONTENTS

Month 1

The Secret of the Abiding Presence

Day 1

1/1/18

The Abiding Presence

"I am with you always, even to the end of the age." (Matt. 28:20)

WHEN the Lord chose His twelve disciples, it was "that they should be with Him, and that He might send them forth to preach" (Mark 3:14). A life in fellowship with Him prepared them for the work of preaching.

So deeply were the disciples conscious of this great privilege, that when Christ spoke of His leaving them to go to the Father their hearts were filled with great sorrow. The presence of Christ had become indispensable to them; they could not think of living without Him. To comfort them, Christ gave them the promise of the Holy Spirit, assuring them of His heavenly presence in a sense far deeper and more intimate than they ever had known on earth. The law of their first calling remained unchanged: their unbroken fellowship with Him was the secret of their power to preach and to testify of Him.

When Christ gave them the Great Commission to go into all the world and preach the gospel to every creature, He added the words, "I am with you always, even to the end of the age."

The same principle stands for all His servants, for all time: without the experience of His presence with us, our preaching has no power. The secret of our strength is the living testimony that Jesus Christ is every moment with us, inspiring, directing, and strengthening us. This is what made the disciples so bold in preaching Him as the Crucified One in the midst of His enemies. They never for a moment regretted His bodily absence, for they had Him with them, and in them, in the divine power of the Holy Spirit.

In all the work of the minister and the missionary, everything depends on the consciousness, through a living faith, of the abiding presence of the Lord with His servant. The living experience of the presence of Jesus is an essential element in preaching the gospel. If this becomes clouded, work becomes a human effort, without the freshness and power of the heavenly life. Nothing can bring back the power and blessing but a return to the Master's feet so that He may breathe into the heart, in divine power, His blessed word, "I am with you always!"

Day 2
11/2/18

The Omnipotence of Christ

"All authority has been given to Me in heaven and on earth." (Matt. 28:18)

BEFORE Christ gave His disciples the Great Commission, to bring His gospel to every creature, He first revealed Himself in His divine power as a partner with God Himself, the Almighty One. It was their faith in this that enabled the disciples to undertake the work in all simplicity and boldness. They had begun to know Him in that mighty resurrection power which had conquered sin and death; there was nothing too great for Him to command or for them to undertake.

Every disciple of Jesus Christ who desires to take part in the victory that overcomes the world needs time, faith, and the Holy Spirit to convince him that, as the servant of the omnipotent Lord Jesus, he is to take part in the work. He is to count literally upon the daily experience of being "strong in the Lord and in the power of His might" (Eph. 6:10). The word of promise gives the courage to obey implicitly the word of command.

Just think of what the disciples had come to know of the power of Christ Jesus here on earth! Yet that was a little thing compared to the greater works that He was now to do in and through them (John 14:12). He has the power to work even in the feeblest of His servants with the strength of the almighty God. He has power even to use their apparent impotence to carry out His purposes. He has the power over every enemy and every human heart, over every difficulty and danger.

But remember that this power is never meant to be experienced as if it were our own. It is only as Jesus Christ as a living Person dwells and works with His divine energy in our own hearts and lives that there can be power in our preaching as a personal testimony. When Christ said to Paul, "My strength is made perfect in weakness" (2 Cor. 12:9), Paul could say what he had never learned to say before: "When I am weak, then am I strong" (12:10). The disciple of Christ who understands that all power has been entrusted by the Father to Jesus Christ, to be received from Him hour by hour, will feel the need and experience the power of that precious word, "I am with you always" — I, the Almighty One.

Day 3

The Omnipresence of Christ

"I will certainly be with you." (Ex. 3:12)

THE first thing that comes to a human's mind when thinking of a god is power, however limited. And the first thought about the true God is His omnipotence: "I am God Almighty." The second thought in Scripture is His omnipresence. God promises His servants that His unseen presence is with them. To His "I am with you," their faith responds, "You are with me."

When Christ said to His disciples, "All authority [power, KJV] has been given to Me in heaven and on earth" (Matt. 28:18), He immediately followed with the promise, "I am with you always" (28:20). The Omnipotent One is surely the Omnipresent One.

The writer of Psalm 139 speaks of God's omnipresence as something beyond his comprehension: "Such knowledge is too wonderful for me; it is high, I cannot attain it" (139:6).

The revelation of God's omnipresence in the man Christ Jesus makes the mystery still deeper. It also makes the grace that enables us to claim this presence as our strength and our joy something inexpressibly blessed. Yet many a servant of Christ finds it difficult to understand all that is implied in this promise and how it can become his daily, practical experience.

Here, as elsewhere in the spiritual life, everything depends on faith — accepting Christ's word as a divine reality and trusting the Holy Spirit to make it true to us from moment to moment. When Christ says "always" (literally, "all the days"), He means to assure us that we need not have a day of our life without that blessed presence with us. And "all the days" implies, also, "all the day." There need not be a moment without that presence. It does not depend on what we do, but on what He does. The omnipotent Christ is the omnipresent Christ; the ever-present is the everlasting, unchangeable One. And as surely as He is the unchangeable One, His presence — the power of an endless life — will be with each of His servants who trusts Him for it.

Our attitude must be a quiet, restful faith, a humble, lowly dependence on the word, "Rest in the Lord, and wait patiently for Him" (Ps. 37:7).

"I am with you always." Let our faith in Christ, the Omnipresent One, be in the quiet confidence that He will every day and every moment keep us as the apple of His eye, keep us in perfect peace, and in the sure experience of all the light and the strength we need in His service.

Day 4

Christ the Savior of the World

"This is indeed the Christ, the Savior of the world." (John 4:42)

OMNIPOTENCE and omnipresence are what are called natural attributes of God. They have their true worth only when linked to and inspired by His moral attributes, holiness and love. When our Lord spoke of having been given all power in earth and heaven (omnipotence) and His presence with each of His disciples (omnipresence), His words pointed to that which lies at the root of everything: His divine glory as the Savior of the world and Redeemer of men. It was because He humbled Himself and became obedient to death on a cross that God so highly exalted Him. As the man Christ Jesus, He shared in the attributes of God because of His perfect obedience to the will of God in accomplishing the redemption of man.

This is what gives meaning and worth to what He says of Himself as the omnipotent and omnipresent One. Between His mention of these two attributes, He gives the command to go into all the world and preach the gospel and teach men to obey all that He has commanded. It is as the Redeemer who saves and keeps from sin, as the Lord Christ who claims obedience to all that He has commanded, that He promises His divine presence to be with His servants.

It follows as a matter of necessity that only when His servants show in their lives that they obey Him in all His commands can they expect the fullness of His power and His presence to be with them. Only when they themselves are living witnesses to the reality of His power to save and to keep from sin can they expect to experience His abiding presence, and the power to train others to the life of obedience that He asks.

It is Jesus Christ, the one who saves His people from their sin and enables them to say, "I delight to do Your will, O my God," who says, "I am with you always." The abiding presence of the Savior from sin is promised to all who have accepted Him in the fullness of His redeeming power and who preach by their lives as well as by their words what a wonderful Savior He is.

Day 5

Christ Crucified

But God forbid that I should glory except in the cross of our Lord Jesus Christ, by whom the world has been crucified to me, and I to the world. (Gal. 6:14)

CHRIST'S highest glory is His cross. It was in this that He glorified the Father, and the Father glorified Him. In that wonderful fifth chapter of Revelation, it is the slain Lamb in the midst of the throne who receives the worship of the ransomed and the angels and all creation.

And His servants have learned to say, "God forbid that I should glory except in the cross of our Lord Jesus Christ, by whom the world has been crucified to me, and I to the world" (Gal. 6:14). Is it not reasonable that Christ's highest glory should be our only glory too?

When the Lord Jesus said to His disciples, "I am with you always," it was as the Crucified One, who had shown them His hands and His feet, that He gave this promise. And to each one who seeks to claim His promise, it is of the first importance that he should realize that it is the crucified Jesus who offers to be with me every day.

Could one reason why we find it so difficult to expect and enjoy the abiding presence be because we do not glory in the cross by which we are crucified to the world? We have been crucified with Christ; our "old man is crucified with Him" (Rom. 6:6); "those who are Christ's have crucified the flesh with its passions and desires" (Gal. 5:24). Yet how little we have learned that the world has been crucified to us and that we are free from its power. How little we have learned, as those who are crucified with Christ, to deny ourselves, to have the mind that was in Christ when He emptied Himself and took the form of a servant, then humbled Himself and became obedient even to the death of the cross (Phil. 2:7–8).

Let us learn the lesson that it is the crucified Christ who comes to walk with us every day and in whose power we too are to live the life that can declare, "I have been crucified with Christ; Christ crucified lives in me."

Day 6

Christ Glorified

For the Lamb who is in the midst of the throne will shepherd them. . . . These are the ones who follow the Lamb wherever He goes. (Rev. 7:17; 14:4).

" 'WHO is it who says, "I am with you always" (Matt. 28:20)? If He offers to be with us throughout the day, we must take time to get to know Him, so we can understand what to expect from Him. Who is He? None other than the Lamb that was slain, standing in the center of the throne! The Lamb in His deepest humiliation is now enthroned in the glory of God. This is the one who invites me to have close fellowship with and likeness to Him.

It takes time and calls for deep reverence and adoring worship to fully realize that He who dwells in the glory of the Father, before whom all heaven bows in prostrate adoration, is none other than the One who offers to be my companion, to lead me like a shepherd — a shepherd who cares for each of His sheep — so that I might be one of those who follow the Lamb wherever He goes.

Read and re-read the wonderful fifth chapter of Revelation, until your heart is possessed by this one great thought: all heaven falls prostrate, the elders cast their crowns before the throne, and the Lamb reigns in the midst of the praises and love of His ransomed ones and of all creation.

If this is He who offers to walk with me in my daily life, to be my strength, my joy and my almighty Keeper, surely I cannot expect Him to abide with me unless I bow my heart in a still deeper reverence, if possible, and in surrender to a life of such praise and service as is worthy of the love that has redeemed me.

The Lamb in the center of the throne is the embodiment of the love and omnipotent glory of the everlasting God. With this Lamb of God as your almighty Shepherd and your faithful Keeper, the thoughts and cares of earth need not prevail and separate you from His love for a single moment.

Day 7

The Great Question

"Do you believe that I am able to do this?" They said to Him, "Yes, Lord."
(Matt. 9:28)

I F you can believe, all things are possible to him who believes.' Immediately the father of the child cried out and said with tears, 'Lord, I believe; help my unbelief!'" (Mark 9:23–24). "Jesus said, 'He who believes in Me, though he may die, he shall live. . . . Do you believe this?' She said to Him, 'Yes, Lord, I believe'" (John 11:25–27).

Because of what we have seen and heard of Christ Jesus, our heart is ready, in answer to His question, to say with Martha: "Yes, Lord, I believe that You are the Christ, the Son of God." But when it comes to believing Christ's promise of the power of the resurrection life — of His abiding presence every day and all the day — we do not find it so easy to declare, "I believe that this omnipotent, omnipresent, unchangeable Christ, our Redeemer God, will walk with me all the day, and give me the unceasing consciousness of His holy presence." It seems to be too strong a statement. And yet it is just this faith for which Christ asks and which He is waiting to work within us.

We need to clearly understand the conditions under which Christ offers to reveal to us the secret of His abiding presence. God cannot force His blessings on us against our will. He seeks in every possible way to stir our desire and help us realize that He is able and willing to fulfill His promises. The resurrection of Christ from the dead is His great plea, His all-prevailing argument. If He can raise Christ, who died under the burden of all our sin and curse, surely He can, now that Christ has conquered death and is to us the Resurrection and the Life, fulfill in our hearts His promise that Christ can be so with us and so in us that He Himself is our life all the day.

So now the great question comes: In view of what we have said and seen about Christ as our Lord, as our redeeming God, are we willing to take His word in all simplicity in its divine fullness of meaning and to rest in the promise, "I am with you all the day"? Christ's question comes to us individually: "Do you believe this?" Let us not rest until we have bowed before Him and said, "Yes, Lord, I believe."

Day 8

Christ Manifesting Himself

"He who has My commandments and keeps them, it is he who loves Me. And he who loves Me will be loved by My Father, and I will love him and manifest Myself to him."
(John 14:21)

CHRIST promised the disciples that the Holy Spirit would come to reveal His continual presence with them. When the Spirit came, Christ manifested Himself to them through the Spirit. They knew Him in a new, divine, spiritual way; they knew Him in the power of the Spirit, and had Him far more intimately and unceasingly with them than they ever had upon earth.

The condition of this revelation of Himself is comprised in the one word love: "He who has My commandments and keeps them, it is he who loves Me: and he who loves Me will be loved of My Father, and I will love him." It is the meeting of divine and human love. The love with which Christ loved them had taken possession of their hearts and would show itself in a love characterized by full and absolute obedience. The Father would see this, and His love would rest upon that soul. Christ would then love him with the special love drawn out by the loving heart and would manifest Himself. The love of heaven shed abroad in the heart would be met by a new and blessed revelation of Christ Himself.

But this is not all. When the question was asked, "Lord, how is it that You will manifest Yourself to us?" (14:22), the answer came in the repetition of the words, "If anyone loves Me, he will keep My word"; and then again, "My Father will love him, and We will come to him and make Our home with him" (14:23). In the heart thus prepared by the Holy Spirit, showing itself in the obedience of love in a fully surrendered life, the Father and the Son will take up residence.

And now, nothing less is what Christ promises them: "I am with you always." "With" implies "in" — Christ with the Father, dwelling in the heart by faith. I wish that everyone who wanted to enter into the secret of the abiding presence — "I am with you always" — would study, believe, and claim in childlike simplicity the blessed promise, "I will manifest Myself to him."

Day 9

Mary: the Morning Watch

Jesus said to her, "Mary!" She turned and said to Him, "Rabboni!" (which is to say, Teacher). (John 20:16)

HERE we have the first manifestation of the risen Savior to Mary Magdalene, the woman who loved much.

Think of what the morning watch meant to Mary. It is proof of the intense longing of her love that she would not rest until she had found the Lord. It meant separating herself from everyone else, even from the chief of the apostles, in her longing to find Christ. It meant struggling against fear with a faith that refused to let go of the wonderful promise. It meant that Christ came and fulfilled the promise: "If anyone loves Me, he will keep My word . . . and I will love him and manifest Myself to him" (John 14:23, 21). It meant that her love was met by the love of Jesus, and she found Him, the living Lord, in all the power of His resurrection life. It meant that she now understood what He had said about ascending to the Father, to the life of divine and omnipotent glory. It meant, too, that she received marching orders from her Lord to go and tell His brethren what she had heard from Him.

That first morning watch of the disciples, as they waited for the risen Lord to reveal Himself (Matt. 28:16), was a prophecy and pledge of what a morning devotional time is for many of us. In fear and doubt, yet with a burning love and strong hope, they waited until He whom they had barely known (because of their feeble human minds) breathed on them in the power of His resurrection life and manifested Himself as the Lord of glory. There they learned, not in words or thought but in the reality of a divine experience, what it meant to have the One who had been given all power in earth and heaven as an abiding presence.

And what are we now to learn? That nothing is a greater attraction to our Lord than the love that sacrifices everything and is satisfied with nothing less than Himself. It is to such a love that Christ manifests Himself. He loved us and gave Himself for us. Christ's love needs our love in which to reveal itself. It is to our love that He speaks the word: "I am with you always." It is love that accepts and rejoices in and lives in that word.

Day 10

Emmaus: the Evening Prayer

But they constrained Him, saying, "Abide with us"... And He went in to stay with them.... [and] He took bread, blessed and broke it, and gave it to them. Then their eyes were opened, and they knew Him. (Luke 24:29–31)

IF Mary teaches us how the morning watch can reveal Jesus to us, the two disciples on the Emmaus road in Luke 24 remind us of the place that evening prayer can have in preparing for the full manifestation of Christ in the soul.

To these disciples, the day had begun in thick darkness. When the women told of seeing an angel who said Jesus was alive, they didn't know what to think. When "Jesus Himself drew near" their eyes were "restrained" and they didn't recognize Him. How often Jesus comes near to show Himself to us, but we are so slow of heart to believe what the Word has declared.

But as the Lord spoke with them their hearts began to burn within them, even though they never thought it might be Him. It is often the same today: the Word becomes precious to us in the fellowship of the saints; our hearts are stirred with a new vision of what Christ's presence may be, and yet our eyes are restrained, and we fail to see Him.

When the Lord acted as though He would have gone farther, their request, "Abide with us," constrained Him. Christ had given, in the last night, a new meaning to the word "Abide." They did not yet understand that, but in their use of it they received far more than they expected — a foretaste of the life of abiding which the resurrection now made possible.

We need to learn to pause toward the close of the day, perhaps leaving the fellowship of others, and with our whole heart take up anew the promise of the abiding presence, praying with an urgency that constrains Jesus — "Abide with us."

What is now the chief lesson of this story? What led our Lord to reveal Himself to these two men? Nothing less than this: their intense devotion to their Lord. Despite our ignorance and unbelief, if we have a burning desire that longs for Him above everything else, a desire that is fostered by the Word, we may count on Him to make Himself known to us. To such intense devotion and constraining prayer the Lord's message will be given in power: "I am with you always." Our eyes will be opened, and we will know Him and the blessed secret of the always-abiding presence. It is to strong desire and constraining prayer that Christ is certain to reveal Himself.

Day 11

The Disciples: Their Divine Mission

Then, the same day at evening . . . when the doors were shut where the disciples were assembled, for fear of the Jews, Jesus came and stood in the midst, and said to them, "Peace be with you." (John 20:19)

THE disciples had received the message of Mary. Peter also said that he had seen the Lord. Late in the evening the men from Emmaus told how He had been made known to them. Their hearts were prepared for what now came, when Jesus stood in their midst and said, "Peace be with you," and showed them His hands and feet. This was not only a sign of recognition; it was also the deep eternal mystery of what would be seen in heaven when He was exalted to the throne: "a Lamb as though it had been slain" (Rev. 5:6).

John goes on to say that "the disciples were glad when they saw the Lord" (20:20). And He spoke again: "Peace to you! As the Father has sent Me, I also send you" (20:21). With Mary, He had revealed Himself to the fervent love that could not rest without Him. With the men at Emmaus it was their constraining prayer that received the revelation. Here, now, He meets the willing servants whom He had trained for His service and hands over to them the work He had done on earth. He changes their fear into the boldness of peace and gladness. He later on ascends to the Father; the work the Father had given Him to do He entrusts to them. The divine mission is now theirs to make known and carry out to victory.

For this divine work they will need nothing less than divine power. He breathes upon them the resurrection life He had won by His death. He fulfills the promise He gave: "Because I live, you will live also" (John 14:19). The exceeding greatness of the mighty power of God by which He raised Christ from the dead — none other than that Spirit of holiness by which He, as the Son of God, was resurrected — will now work in them! And all that is bound or loosed by them in that power will be bound or loosed in heaven.

The story comes to every messenger of the gospel with soul-stirring force. To us, too, the word has been spoken: "As the Father has sent Me, I also send you." For us, too, is the word "Receive the Holy Spirit" (John 20:22); for us, too, is Jesus revealed as the Living One, with the pierced hands and feet. If our hearts are set on nothing less than the presence of the living Lord, we may confidently count that it will be given to us. Jesus never sends His servants out without the promise of His abiding presence and His almighty power.

Day 12

Thomas: the Blessedness of Believing

Jesus said to him, "Thomas, because you have seen Me, you have believed. Blessed are those who have not seen and yet have believed." (John 20:29)

WE all think Thomas received a wonderful blessing: Christ appeared and allowed Thomas to touch His hands and side. No wonder he could find no words but those of holy adoration: "My Lord and my God" (John 20:28). Has there ever been a higher expression of the overwhelming nearness and glory of God?

And yet Christ said: "Because you have seen Me, you have believed. Blessed are those who have not seen and yet have believed." True, living faith gives a sense of Christ's divine nearness far deeper and more intimate than even the joy that filled the heart of Thomas. Here and now, after all these centuries, we can experience the presence and power of Christ in a far deeper reality than Thomas did. To those who have not seen, yet believe — simply, only, truly, fully believe in what Christ is and can be to them every moment — He has promised to reveal Himself, and the Father and He will come and dwell in them.

How often have you been inclined to think of a "full life of faith" as something beyond your reach? Such a thought robs you of the power to believe. Instead, take hold of Christ's word: "Blessed are those who have not seen, and yet believe." This is a heavenly blessing that fills the whole heart and life — a faith that receives the love and the presence of the living Lord.

How do you obtain this childlike faith? The answer is very simple: If Jesus Christ is the sole object of your desire and your confidence, He will reveal Himself in divine power. Thomas had already proved his intense devotion to Christ when he said, "Let us also go, that we may die with Him" (John 11:16). To such a love, even when it is struggling with unbelief, Jesus Christ will reveal Himself. He will make His holy promise "I am with you always" an actual reality in our conscious experience. See to it that your faith in His blessed word, His divine power, and His holy, abiding presence is the one thing that masters your whole being. Then Christ is sure to reveal Himself, abide with you, and dwell in your heart as His home.

Day 13

Peter: the Greatness of Love

Peter was grieved because He said to him the third time, "Do you love Me?" And he said to Him, "Lord, You know all things; You know that I love You." Jesus said to him, "Feed My sheep." (John 21:17)

IT was to Mary who "loved much" that Christ first revealed Himself. Likewise, when He appeared to Peter, to the two disciples in the supper room at Emmaus, to the ten, and to Thomas, it was always to the intense devotion of prepared hearts that Christ revealed Himself. And in His second appearance to Peter, love is again the keynote.

We can easily understand why Christ asked the question, "Do you love Me?" three times. It was to remind Peter of the terrible self-confidence in which he had said, "Even if I have to die with You, I will not deny You" (Matt. 26:35). It was because of his need for quiet, deep heart-searching before he could be sure that his love was real and true. It was because he needed to be deeply penitent and realize how little he could trust himself. Love was the one thing Peter needed to be fully restored to his place in the heart of Jesus — the first and highest requirement for feeding His sheep and caring for His lambs.

God is love. Christ is the Son of His love. Having loved His own, He loved them to the uttermost, and said: "As the Father loves Me, so love I you." He asked them to prove their love to Him by keeping His commandments and loving each other with the love with which He loved them. In heaven and on earth, in the Father and in the Son, in us and all our work for Him, and especially in our care for souls, the greatest thing is love.

To everyone who longs to have Jesus reveal Himself — as in "I am with you always" — the essential requirement is love. Peter teaches us that such love is not in our power to offer. It comes to us through the power of Christ's death to sin, and of His resurrection life. As he puts it in his first epistle, "Whom having not seen you love. Though now you do not see Him, yet believing, you rejoice with joy inexpressible and full of glory" (1 Pet. 1:8). Thank God, if Peter, the self-confident, could be so changed, can we not believe that Christ will work this wondrous change in us, too? He reveals Himself to a loving heart in all the fullness of His precious declaration, "I am with you always." It is to love that Christ reveals Himself, and only those who love are fit to feed His sheep and tend His lambs.

Day 14

John: Life from the Dead

And when I saw Him, I fell at His feet as dead. But He laid His right hand on me, saying to me, "Do not be afraid; I am the First and the Last. I am He who lives, and was dead, and behold, I am alive forevermore. Amen." (Rev. 1:17–18)

HERE we see, sixty or more years after the resurrection, Christ revealing Himself to the beloved disciple. John fell as dead at His feet. When Moses prayed, "Show me Your glory," God said, "You cannot see My face; for no man shall see Me, and live" (Ex. 33:18, 20). Man's sinful nature cannot receive the vision of the divine glory and live; it needs the death of the natural life for the life of God in glory to enter in. When John fell as dead at Christ's feet, it proved how little he could endure the wonderful heavenly vision.

When Christ laid His right hand upon him and said, "Do not be afraid . . . I am He who lives, and was dead, and behold, l am alive forevermore," He reminded him that He Himself, too, had passed through death before He could rise to the life and the glory of God. For the Master Himself and for every disciple, for Moses and for John, there is only one way to the glory of God: death to all that has been in contact with sin and cannot enter heaven.

The lesson is a deep and necessary one for all who long for Jesus to reveal Himself to them. Deep knowledge of Jesus — fellowship with Him and the experience of His power — is not possible without sacrificing all that is in us of the world and its spirit. The disciples had personal experience of this. From His first ordination charge, where He spoke about forsaking father and mother, taking up the cross, and losing our life for His sake (Matt. 10:37–39), down to the days before His death, when He said, "Unless a grain of wheat falls into the ground and dies, it remains alone; but if it dies, it produces much grain," and "He who loves his life will lose it" (John 12:24), Christ made this His one great command: deny yourself, bear the cross, and follow Me.

The secret of having the Lord Jesus' daily abiding presence is accepting the principle of "through death to life." In the power of Christ Jesus — with whom we have been crucified, and whose death now works in us if we yield ourselves to it — *death* to sin and to the world, with all its self-pleasing and self-exaltation, must be the deepest law of our spiritual life. Peter advised Jesus to spare Himself from the cross (Matt. 16:22). Jesus said to him, "Deny yourself." The disciples followed Christ even to the cross. That was what made them fit to receive the Master's word, "I am with you always."

Day 15

Paul: Christ Revealed in Him

But . . . it pleased God . . . to reveal His Son in me. (Gal. 1:15–16)

IN all our study and worship of Christ, five points come to mind: the Incarnate Christ, the Crucified Christ, the Enthroned Christ, the Indwelling Christ, and Christ Coming in Glory. The first is the seed, the second the seed cast into the ground, and the third the seed growing up to heaven. The fourth is the fruit: Christ dwelling in the heart through the Holy Spirit. The fifth is the gathering of the fruit when Christ appears.

Paul tells us that it pleased God to reveal His Son in him (Gal. 1:15–16). And he gives his testimony of that revelation: "Christ lives in me" (Gal. 2:20). The main aspect of that life, he says, is that he is crucified with Christ and is able to say, "I no longer live." In Christ he had found the death of self.

Just as the cross is the chief characteristic of Christ Himself — "A lamb as though it had been slain" (Rev. 5:6) — so the life of Christ in Paul made him inseparably one with his crucified Lord. So completely was this the case that he could say, "But God forbid that I should glory except in the cross of our Lord Jesus Christ, by whom the world has been crucified to me, and I to the world" (Gal. 6:14).

Suppose you had asked Paul, "If Christ actually lives in you, so that you no longer live, what becomes of your responsibility?" His answer was ready and clear: "I live by faith in the Son of God, who loved me and gave Himself for me" (Gal. 2:20). Every moment he lived was a life of faith in the One who loved him and gave Himself so completely that He had undertaken at all times to be the life of His willing disciple.

This was the sum and substance of all Paul's preaching. He asks for intercession that he might proclaim "this mystery among the Gentiles: which is Christ in you, the hope of glory" (Col. 1:27). The indwelling Christ was the secret of his life of faith; the one power, the one aim of all his life and work; the hope of glory. We can be sure that the abiding presence of Christ is given to everyone who trusts Him fully.

Day 16

Why Could We Not?

*Then the disciples came to Jesus privately and said, "Why could we not cast him out?"
So Jesus said to them, "Because of your unbelief. . . . However, this kind does not go
out except by prayer and fasting." (Matt. 17:19–21)*

T HE disciples had often cast out demons, but now they had been unable
to do so. They asked the Lord what the reason might be. His answer is
very simple: "Because of your unbelief."

We have here the reply to the great question so often asked, "How is it that
we cannot live that life of unbroken fellowship with Christ which the Scripture
promises?" Simply, because of our unbelief. We do not realize that faith must
accept and expect that God will, by His almighty power, fulfill every promise
He has made. We do not live in that utter helplessness and dependence on God
alone which is the very essence of faith. We are not strong in our faith, fully
persuaded that what God has promised He is able and willing to perform. We
do not give ourselves with our whole heart simply to believe that God by His
almighty power will work wonders in our hearts.

But what is the reason that this faith is so often lacking? "However, this
kind does not go out except by prayer and fasting." To have a strong faith in
God demands a life in close touch with Him by persistent prayer. We cannot
call up faith on our own; it requires close intercourse with God. It requires not
only prayer but fasting too, in the larger and deeper meaning of that word. It
requires the denial of self — giving up "the lust of the flesh, the lust of the eyes,
and the pride of life" (1 John 2:16), which is the essence of a worldly spirit. To
gain the prizes of the heavenly life here on earth calls for the sacrifice of all that
earth can offer. Just as it takes God to satisfy the human heart and work His
mighty miracles in it, it takes the whole man, utterly given up to God, to have
the faith which can cast out every evil spirit. "Prayer and fasting" are essential.

Day 17

The Power of Obedience

"And He who sent Me is with Me. The Father has not left Me alone, for I always do those things that please Him." (John 8:29)

IN these words Christ not only tells what *His* life with the Father was like, but reveals at the same time the law of *all* intercourse with God — simple obedience.

How strongly He insisted upon it is seen in His Farewell Discourse (John 14–16). In chapter 14 He says three times that loving Him means keeping His commandments (14:15, 21, 23). And likewise three times over in chapter 15 he connects our love to Him with abiding in His word, or obeying Him (15:7, 10, 14).

Obedience is the proof and practice of the love of God that has been poured out in our hearts by the Holy Spirit. Obedience comes from love and leads to love — a deeper and a fuller experience of God's love and indwelling. It assures us that what we ask will be given to us. It assures us that we are abiding in the love of Christ. It seals our claim to be called the friends of Christ. And so it is not only a proof of love but of faith too, since we are promised that "whatever we ask we receive from Him, because we keep His commandments and do those things that are pleasing in His sight" (1 John 3:22).

To have the abiding enjoyment of His holy presence, simple, full obedience is necessary. The new covenant has made full provision for this: "I will . . . write [My law] on their hearts" (Jer. 31:33); "I will put My fear in their hearts, so that they will not depart from Me" (Jer. 32:40); "I will put My Spirit within you and cause you to walk in My statutes, and you will keep My judgments and do them" (Ezek. 36:27).

Blessed obedience, that enables us to abide in His love and gives the full experience of His unbroken presence! Christ did not speak of an impossibility; He saw what we might confidently expect in the power of the Spirit. Let this thought take deep hold of you: to the obedient comes the promise, "I am with you always," and to them all the fullness of its meaning will be revealed.

Day 18

The Power of Intercession

"We will give ourselves continually to prayer." (Acts 6:4)
Constant prayer was offered to God for him by the church. (Acts 12:5)

WHILE traveling in Asia, Dr. John R. Mott was urged by missionaries there to remind us of the imperative need for more intercession — above all, of united intercession.

"We can in no way better serve the deepest interest of the churches than by multiplying the number of real intercessors, and by focusing the prayers of Christendom upon those great situations which demand the almighty working of the Spirit of God," Dr. Mott said. "Far more important and vital than any service we can render to missions is that of helping to release the superhuman energy of prayer, and, through uniting true intercessors of all lands in this holy ministry, to help usher in a new era abounding in signs and wonders. . . . Immeasurably more important than any other work is the linking of all we do to the fountain of divine life and energy."

And where is there a greater need of focusing the united intercession of Christendom than on the great army of missionaries? They confess the need of the presence and the power of God's Spirit in their life and work. They long for the experience of the abiding presence and the power of Christ every day. They need it; they have a right to it. Will you be a part of that great army which pleads with God for that enduement of power which is so absolutely necessary for effective work? Will you, like the early apostles, "continue steadfastly in prayer" until God sends an abundant answer?

As we give ourselves continually to prayer, the power of Christ's promise, "I am with you always," will be proved in our lives and in theirs.

Day 19

The Power of Time

My times are in Your hand. (Psalm 31:15)

THE plural implies the singular: "My time is in Your hand. It belongs to You; You alone have a right to command it. I yield it wholly and gladly to Your disposal." What mighty power time can exert if wholly given up to God!

Time is the lord of all things. What is the history of the world but a proof of how, slowly but surely, time has made man what he is today? All around us we see the proof — in the growth of a child to physical and mental adulthood, in the success of every pursuit, in all our endeavors and attainments. All these are under the law of time and its inconceivable power over how we spend our lives.

This is especially true in spiritual matters and one's intercourse with God. Time here, too, is master. What glorious fellowship with God! What holiness and blessedness! What likeness to His image and what power in His service for blessing to men! All these benefits we can obtain on one condition: that we have sufficient time with God for His holiness to shine on us with its light and heat and make us partakers of His Spirit and His life. The very essence of religion lies in the concept of time with God.

And yet many of God's servants, even while giving their lives to His service, frankly admit to feebleness in their spiritual life and to inadequate results in their work as a whole, due to a failure to set aside time and use it rightly in daily communion with God.

The cause behind this sad situation is nothing but a lack of faith — a failure to believe that time spent alone with God truly will bring power into our lives and enable us to use our time wisely and enjoy His abiding presence with us all the day.

If you are complaining that overwork, or too much zeal in doing the work, is hindering your spiritual efficiency, submit your timetable to the inspection of Christ and His Holy Spirit, and you will find that a new life will be yours. You must fully believe and then put into daily practice the word, "My time is in Your hand."

Day 20

The Power of Faith

"All things are possible to him who believes." (Mark 9:23)

THERE is no truth that Christ insisted on more frequently, both with His disciples and with strangers who came seeking His help, than the absolute necessity of faith, with its unlimited possibilities. And experience has taught us that there is nothing in which we fall so short as a simple and absolute trust in God to fulfill literally, in us, all that He has promised. To have a life in the abiding presence requires a life of unceasing faith.

Think for a moment of what the marks of true faith are. First of all, faith counts on God to do all He has promised. It is not content with taking hold of some promises; it seeks nothing less than to claim every promise that God has made and does so in its largest and fullest meaning. Sensing its own nothingness and utter impotence, it trusts the power of an almighty God to work His wonders in the heart in which He dwells.

It does this wholeheartedly and with all its strength. Faith yields to the promise that God will take full possession of the believer and, all through the day and night, fulfill his hope and expectation. It recognizes the inseparable link between God's promises and His commands, and submits to doing the one as fully as it trusts the other.

In pursuit of the power which such a life of faith can give, there is often a faith that seeks and strives, but cannot grasp. This is then followed by a faith that begins to see the need to wait on God, and it quietly rests in the hope of what God will do. This should lead to an act of decision in which the soul takes God at His word and claims the fulfillment of the promise, looking to Him even in utter darkness to perform what He has spoken.

The kind of faith which leads to the abiding presence demands a mastery of one's whole being. Experiencing Christ's presence all day long is such a wonderful privilege that it calls us to forsake many things we formerly thought were lawful. The blessed Friend who accompanies us, the joy and light of our life, must be Lord of all. Then faith will be able to claim and experience the words of the Master, "I am with you always."

Day 21

John's Missionary Message

That which we have seen and heard we declare to you, that you also may have fellowship with us; and truly our fellowship is with the Father and with His Son Jesus Christ. (1 John 1:3)

WHAT a revelation of the calling of the preacher of the gospel! His message is nothing less than to proclaim that Christ has opened the way for us simple men to have daily, living, loving fellowship with the holy God! He is to preach this as a witness to the life he himself lives in all its blessed experience. In the power of that testimony he is to prove its reality, and to show how a sinful man upon earth can indeed live in fellowship with the Father and the Son.

The message suggests that the very first duty of a pastor or missionary is to maintain such close communion with God that he can preach the truth in fullness of joy, and with a consciousness that his life and conversation are proof that his preaching is true, so that his words appeal with power to the heart. "And these things we write to you that your joy may be full" (1 John 1:4).

In an article in *The International Review of Missions* of October 1914, on the influence of the Keswick Convention on mission work, the substance of Keswick teaching is given in these words: "It points to a life of communion with God through Christ as a reality to be entered upon, and constantly maintained, by the unconditional and habitual surrender of the whole personality to Christ's control and government, in the assurance that the living Christ will take possession of the life thus yielded to Him." It is such teaching, revealing the infinite claim and power of Christ's love as maintained by the power of the Holy Spirit, that will encourage and compel men to make the measure of Christ's surrender for them the only measure of their surrender to Him and His service.

It is this intimate fellowship with Christ (as the secret of daily service and testimony) that has power to make Christ known as the deliverer from sin and the inspiration of a life of wholehearted devotion to His service.

This intimate and abiding fellowship with Christ is promised in the verse "I am with you always" (Matt. 28:20). This is what every missionary needs, and has a right to claim. This alone maintains that spiritual efficiency which will influence the workers and converts with whom he comes in contact.

Day 22

Paul's Missionary Message

*Continue earnestly in prayer . . . meanwhile praying also for us, that God would open
to us a door for the word, to speak the mystery of Christ . . . that I may
make it manifest, as I ought to speak. (Col. 4:2–4)*

*The mystery which has been hidden . . . but now has been revealed to His saints.
To them God willed to make known what are the riches of the glory of this mystery
among the Gentiles: which is Christ in you, the hope of glory. (Col. 1:26–27)*

TO Paul, the very center and substance of his gospel was the indwelling
Christ. He spoke of "the riches of the glory of this mystery . . . Christ in
you, the hope of glory." Though he had been so many years a preacher of this
gospel, he still asked for prayer, that he might make known that mystery clearly.

A complaint often made of churches on the mission field is that, after a
time, there appears to be no further growth, and very little joy and power for
bearing witness to Christ Jesus. The question to be asked is whether the missionary's church at home is living in the experience of this indwelling Christ.
If not, how can the sons and daughters this church sends out know the secret
and make it the substance of their teaching and preaching?

Some years ago, one of our workers returned from the mission field to do
deputation work. Before he began visiting the supporting churches, there was
a little gathering for prayer at which he asked what his general message should
be. The thought was expressed that since he would be speaking to Christians,
it was desirable that a message of a full salvation should be pressed home and
hearts be roused to believe in an indwelling Christ. Upon his return, he told
what deep interest the presentation of this truth had produced; many people
said they had never before rightly understood it.

Dr. Alexander Maclaren said years ago that "it seems as if the Church has
lost the truth of the indwelling Christ." We speak of Paul's missionary methods,
but is there not a greater need of Paul's missionary message, which culminates
in the phrase, "Christ in you, the hope of glory"? Even Paul felt a great need for
prayer to enable him to give the message correctly. All missionary intercessors,
and our beloved missionaries themselves, should make it their top priority to
obtain the power, growing from personal experience, to lead Christians into the
enjoyment of their rightful heritage. And it may be that the Church at home
will also share in the blessing — the restoration of the truth, "Christ in you,
the hope of glory" to its rightful place.

Day 23

The Missionary's Life

You are witnesses, and God also, how devoutly and justly and blamelessly we behaved ourselves among you who believe. (1 Thess. 2:10)

PAUL more than once appeals to what his converts had seen in his own life. So he says, "For our boasting is this: the testimony of our conscience that we conducted ourselves in the world in simplicity and godly sincerity, not with fleshly wisdom but by the grace of God, and more abundantly toward you" (2 Cor. 1:12). Christ, also, had taught His disciples as much by His life as by His teaching. Paul consistently sought to be a living witness to the truth of all that he had preached about Christ — as able to save and to keep from sin, as renewing the whole nature by the power of His Holy Spirit, as Himself becoming the life of those who believe in Him.

In the *W. M. C. Report* (Vol. v, p. 217) one finds this statement: "It has come to pass that our representatives on the field, just because they are what we have made them, have far too often hidden the Christ whom they are giving their lives to reveal. It is only in proportion as the missionary can manifest the character of Christ in and through his own life that he can gain a hearing for the gospel. Only as far as he can live Christ before their eyes can he help them to understand his message."

Paul's appeal to his own holy, righteous and blameless life gave him courage to put a high standard before his converts in Thessalonica. He calls on them to trust God to establish their hearts blameless in holiness before God (1 Thess. 3:13). And in Philippians 4:9 he writes, "The things which you . . . heard and saw in me, these do, and the God of peace will be with you." Then to Timothy he declares, "And the grace of our Lord was exceedingly abundant, with faith and love which are in Christ Jesus . . . a pattern to those who are going to believe on Him for everlasting life" (1 Tim. 1:14, 16).

When Paul said, "Christ lives in me, I live no more," he spoke of an actual, divine, unceasing abiding of Christ in him, working in him from hour to hour all that was pleasing to the Father. Do not rest until you can say, "The Christ of Paul is my Christ! His missionary standard is mine, too!"

Day 24

The Holy Spirit

"He will glorify Me, for He will take of what is Mine and declare it to you."
(John 16:14)

WHEN our Lord said to the disciples, "I am with you always," they did not at first understand or experience His full meaning.

It was only later, at Pentecost, when they were filled with the Holy Spirit and that Spirit from heaven brought down into their hearts the glorified Lord Jesus, that they could begin their new life in the joy of the abiding presence.

All our attempts to claim that life of continuous, unbroken communion will be in vain unless we too yield ourselves wholly to the power and indwelling of the ever-blessed Spirit.

Throughout the Church of Christ there is an appalling lack of knowledge of and faith in the Spirit — His divine nature, what He can enable us to be, and how completely He demands *full and undisturbed possession* of our whole being. Clearly, the fulfillment of Christ's glorious promises about the Father and Son making their abode in us is subject to one essential and indispensable condition — a life utterly and unceasingly yielded to the rule and leading of the Spirit of Christ.

Let no one say, "The experience of Christ's being with us every day and all the day is impossible." Christ meant His word to be a simple and eternal *reality*. He meant these promises — "He who loves Me will be loved by My Father, and I will love him, and will manifest Myself to him," and "We will come unto him and make Our abode with him" — to be accepted as *absolute*, divine truth. But this truth can only be experienced where the Spirit, in His power as God, is known and believed in and obeyed.

What Christ speaks of in John 14 is exactly what Paul testifies to when he says, "Christ lives in me," or, as John expressed it, "By this we know that we abide in Him, and He in us, because He has given us of His Spirit" (1 John 4:13).

Christ came as God to make known the Father, and the Spirit has come as God to make known the Son in us. We need to understand that the Spirit of God not only seeks our absolute subjection but desires, by taking possession of our whole being, to enable us to fulfill all that Christ asks of us. It is the *Spirit* who can deliver us from all the power of the flesh and who can conquer the power of the world. *He* is the One through whom Christ Jesus will reveal Himself to us in nothing less than His abiding presence: "I am with you always."

Day 25

Filled with the Spirit

Be filled with the Spirit, speaking to one another in psalms and hymns and spiritual songs, singing and making melody in your heart to the Lord, giving thanks always for all things. (Eph. 5:18–20)

IF the expression "filled with the Spirit" related only to the story of Pentecost, we might naturally think that it was something special and not meant for ordinary life. But the text above teaches us the great lesson that it is meant for every Christian and for everyday life.

To realize this more fully, think of the Holy Spirit in Christ Jesus and the conditions under which He, as man, was filled with the Spirit. He received the Spirit while praying, having yielded Himself as a sacrifice to God by going down into the sinner's baptism. And full of the Holy Spirit He was led to forty days of fasting, sacrificing the needs of the body in order to be free for fellowship with the Father and have victory over Satan. He even refused, while hungry, to listen to the urging of the Evil One to use His power to make bread. And so He was led by the Spirit through life until He, by the Eternal Spirit, on Calvary offered Himself, without blemish, to God.

For Christ, the Spirit's filling meant prayer, obedience, and sacrifice. If we are to follow Christ — to have His mind in us and live out His life — we must seek to regard the fullness of the Spirit as a daily supply, as a daily provision. Only in this way can we live a life of obedience, joy, self-sacrifice, and power for service. There may be occasions when the fullness of the Spirit is especially evident, but being led by the Spirit — every day and all day — is the only way we can abide in Christ Jesus, conquer the flesh and the world, and live life with God and our fellow men in humble, holy, fruitful service.

Only when we are filled with the Spirit can we fully understand and experience the words of Jesus, "I am with you always." If this seems unattainable, remember that what is impossible with men is possible with God (Luke 18:27). And if we cannot attain to it at once, let us at least make it, in an act of holy decision, our definite aim, our unceasing prayer, our childlike expectation.

"I am with you always" was meant for daily life, with the all-sufficient aid of that blessed Spirit of whom Jesus said, "He who believes in Me . . . out of his heart will flow rivers of living water" (John 7:38). Our faith in Christ is the measure of our fullness of the Spirit. The measure of the power of the Spirit in us will be the measure of our experience of the presence of Christ.

Day 26

The Christl Life

Christ lives in me. (Gal. 2:20)
Christ is our life. (Col. 3:4)

CHRIST'S life was more than His teaching, more than His work, more even than His death. It was His life in the sight of God and man that gave value to what He said and did and suffered. And it is this life, glorified in the resurrection, that He gives to His people, enabling them to live it out before men.

"By this all will know that you are My disciples, if you have love for one another" (John 13:35). It was the life of Christ's Spirit that made both Jews and Greeks feel that there was a superhuman power motivating the new brotherhood that came into being. They gave living proof of the truth of what they said, that God's love had come down and taken possession of them.

It has often been said of the missionary that unless he lives his life on an entirely different level from that on which other men live, he misses the deepest secret of power and success in his work. When Christ sent His disciples forth, it was with the command, "Tarry . . . until you are endued with power from on high" (Luke 24:49). Many a missionary has realized that neither learning, nor zeal, nor a willingness to sacrifice in Christ's service can promise success. It is only the secret experience of a life hidden with Christ in God that enables him to meet and overcome every difficulty.

Everything depends on our life with God in Christ being kept right. It was so with Christ, with the disciples, with Paul. It is the simplicity and intensity of our life in Christ Jesus, and of the life of Christ Jesus in us, that sustains a man in the daily drudgery of work, that makes him conqueror over self and everything that could hinder the Christ-life, and that gives victory over the powers of evil and over the hearts from which the evil spirits have to be cast out.

The life is everything. It was so in Christ Jesus; it must be so in His servants. It can be so, because Christ Himself will live in us. When He spoke the word, "I am with you always," He meant nothing less than this: "Every day and all the day I am with you, the secret of your life, joy, and strength."

There are hidden treasures contained in those blessed words we love to repeat: "I am with you always."

Day 27

The Christ-like Life

Let this mind be in you which was also in Christ Jesus. (Phil. 2:5)

AND what was the mind that was in Christ Jesus? "Who, being in the form of God . . . made Himself of no reputation, taking the form of a servant, and coming in the likeness of men. . . . He humbled Himself and became obedient to the point of death, even the death of the cross" (Phil. 2:6–8). Self-emptying and self-sacrifice, obedience to God's will and submission in love to men, even unto the death of the cross — such was the character of Christ for which God so highly exalted Him. Such is the character of Christ that we are to imitate. He was made in the likeness of men that we might be conformed into the likeness of God.

Self-effacement, self-sacrifice, to do God's will and save man — such was the life of Christ. "Love . . . does not seek its own" (1 Cor. 13:4–5). This was His life: He lived only to please God and to bless men.

This is not an impossibility. "The things which are impossible with men are possible with God" (Luke 18:27). We are called to work out this salvation of a Christ-like character with fear and trembling, for "it is God who works in you both to will and to do for His good pleasure" (Phil. 2:13).

It has been said that "the missionary who is to commend the gospel must first embody it in a character fully conformed to the likeness of Jesus Christ. It is only as far as he can live Christ before the eyes of the converts that he can help them to understand his message. It has at times come to pass that our representatives on the field, just because they are what we have made them, have far too often hidden the Christ whom they are giving their lives to reveal" (*W.M.C. Report*, Vol. v., p. 217).

As the Church aims to make likeness to Christ's character the standard for Christian teachers, our missionaries are able to pass this on to their converts and say to them, as Paul said, "Imitate me, just as I also imitate Christ."

Let us not rest until our faith lays hold of the promise, "It is *God* who works in us." The confidence will be aroused that as the character of Christ is the revelation with which every missionary has been entrusted, so the power will be given to fulfill this high and holy calling. Let ministers and missionaries and all intercessors make this their one great plea and aim: to have this mind that was in Christ Jesus.

Day 28

Christ: the Nearness of God

Draw near to God and He will draw near to you. (James 4:8)

IT has been said that the holiness of God is the union of God's infinite distance from sinful man with God's infinite nearness in His redeeming grace. Faith must always seek to realize both the distance and the nearness.

In Christ, God has come near to man, and James tells us that if we want God to come even nearer, we must draw near to Him. The nearness that Jesus promised when He said, "I am with you always," can only be experienced as we draw near to Him.

That means, first of all, that at the beginning of each day we must yield ourselves afresh for His holy presence to rest upon us. It means a voluntary, intentional and wholehearted turning away from the world, and waiting on God to make Himself known to our souls. It means giving Him time, and all our heart and strength, to allow Him to reveal Himself. We cannot expect to have the abiding presence of Christ with us through the day unless we definitely and daily exercise a strong desire and childlike trust in His word. "Draw near to God, and He will draw near to you."

That also means we must offer ourselves in simple, childlike faith to do His will alone, and to seek above everything to please Him. We can depend on His promise that "If anyone loves Me, he will keep My word; and My Father will love him, and We will come to him and make Our home with him" (John 14:23).

This will bring a quiet assurance, even if there is not much feeling or sense of His presence, that God is with us, and that as we go out to do His will He will watch over us and keep us, strengthening us in the inner man for the work we have to do for Him.

Let these words have a new meaning for you each morning: "Draw near to God, and He will draw near to you." Wait patiently, and He will speak in divine power, "I am with you always."

Day 29

Love

Having loved His own who were in the world, He loved them to the end.
(John 13:1)

THESE are the opening words of that holy, confidential talk of Christ with His disciples in John 13 to 17, as out of the depths of eternity He discoursed with them in the last hours before He went to Gethsemane. They are the revelation and full display of that divine love which was manifested in His death on the cross.

He begins with a new commandment: "Love one another as I have loved you" (13:34). A little later He adds, "If you love Me, keep My commandments. . . . He who . . . loves Me will be loved by My Father, and I will love him and manifest Myself to him. . . . We will come to him and make Our home with him" (14:15, 21, 23). The new, heavenly life in Christ Jesus is to be the unfolding of God's love in Christ.

Further on He says, "As the Father loved Me, I also have loved you; abide in My love. If you keep My commandments, you will abide in My love. . . . This is My commandment, that you love one another as I have loved you. Greater love has no one than this, than to lay down one's life for his friends" (John 15:9–10, 12–13).

Then later He prays "that the world may know that You have sent Me, and have loved them as You have loved Me. . . . I have declared to them Your name . . . that the love with which You loved Me may be in them, and I in them" (John 17:23, 26).

Can His words make it any plainer that God's love to Christ is given that it might pass into us and become our life? That the love with which the Father loved the Son is to be in us? If the Lord Jesus is to reveal Himself to us, it can only be to the loving heart. If we are to claim His daily presence with us, it can only be as a relationship of infinite, tender love between Him and us — love rooted in the fact of God's love to Christ coming into our hearts. And such love will show itself in obedience to His commandment to love one another.

We see how in the early Church the "first love" was forsaken after a time, and confidence was put in all the activities of service (Rev. 2:4). It is only in the atmosphere of a holy, living love that the abiding presence of the loving Christ can be known, and the depth of the divine love expressed in Christ's promise, "I am with you always," can be realized.

Day 30

The Trial and Triumph of Faith

Jesus said to him, "If you can believe, all things are possible to him who believes." Immediately the father of the child cried out and said with tears, "Lord, I believe; help my unbelief!" (Mark 9:23–24)

WHAT a glorious promise: "All things are possible to him who believes"! And yet it is the very greatness of the promise that makes it a trial of faith. At first we do not really believe its truth. But when we have grasped it, then comes the real trial, in which we think, Such a wonder-working faith is utterly beyond my reach.

But the trial of faith soon becomes its triumph! How can this be? When Christ said to the father of the child, "If you can believe, all things are possible to him who believes," he felt that this was only casting him into deeper despair. How could his faith be able to work the miracle? But as he looked into the face of Christ and the love of His tender eyes touched his heart, he felt sure that this blessed Man not only had the power to heal his child but the ability, too, to inspire him with the needed faith. The impression Christ produced upon him made not only the one miracle of the healing possible but the second miracle too — that he should have so great a faith. And with tears he cried, "Lord, I believe; help my unbelief!" The very greatness of faith's trial was the greatness of faith's triumph.

What a lesson! Of all things that are possible to faith, the most impossible is that I should be able to exercise such faith. The abiding presence of Christ is possible to faith. And this faith is possible to the soul that clings to Christ and trusts Him. As surely as He will lead us into His abiding presence all the day, so surely will He strengthen us with divine power for the faith that claims and receives the promise. Blessed is the hour when the believer sees how entirely he is dependent on Christ for the faith as well as the blessing, and, in the consciousness of the unbelief that is still struggling within, he casts himself on the power and the love of Jesus: "Lord, I believe; Lord, I believe!"

Through such trial and through such triumph — sometimes the triumph of despair — we enter upon our inheritance, the abiding presence of Him who speaks to us now: "I am with you always." Let us wait at His feet until we know that He has blessed us. "I can do all things through Christ who strengthens me" (Phil. 4:13).

Day 31

Exceedingly Abundantly

Now to Him who is able to do exceedingly abundantly above all that we ask or think, according to the power that works in us, to Him be glory in the Church by Christ Jesus throughout all ages, world without end. Amen. (Eph. 3:20–21)

IN Paul's great prayer (Eph. 3:14–19), he had apparently reached the highest expression possible regarding the life to which God's mighty power can bring the believer. But Paul is not content. In this doxology he rises still higher and lifts us up to give glory to God as "able to do exceedingly abundantly above all that we ask or think." Pause a moment to think what "exceedingly abundantly" means.

Think of the "exceedingly great and precious promises" (2 Peter 1:4). Think of "the exceeding greatness of His power toward us who believe, according to the working of His mighty power which He worked in Christ when He raised Him from the dead" (Eph. 1:19–20). Think of how "the grace of our Lord was exceedingly abundant, with faith and love which are in Christ Jesus" (1 Tim. 1:14), so that "where sin abounded, grace abounded much more [exceedingly, Gr.]" (Rom. 5:20). Paul now lifts our hearts to give glory to God as "able to do exceedingly abundantly above all that we ask or think, according to the power that works in us" — nothing less than the exceeding greatness of the power that raised Christ from the dead. And when we begin to see the possibility that God will work in us beyond all our imagination, He lifts our hearts to join in the universal chorus: "to Him be glory in the Church by Christ Jesus throughout all ages, world without end. Amen" (Eph 3:21).

As we worship and adore, we are called to believe in this almighty God who is working in our hearts according to His mighty power, able and willing to fulfill every one of His exceedingly great and precious promises and, where sin abounds, to prove that grace abounds more exceedingly.

Paul began his great prayer, "I bow my knees to the Father." He ends it by bringing us to our knees, to give glory to Him as able to fulfill every promise, to reveal Christ as dwelling in our hearts, and to keep us in that life of love which leads to being filled with all the fullness of God.

Child of God, bow in deep adoration, giving glory to God, until your heart learns to believe that the prayer will be fulfilled. Jesus Christ will surely dwell in your heart by faith. Faith in this almighty God and in the exceeding abundance of His grace and power will teach us that the abiding indwelling of Christ in the heart is the secret of the abiding presence.

Month 2

The Secret of Adoration

Day 1

True Worship

"Worship God." (Rev. 22:9)

THOSE who have read the booklet *The Secret of Intercession* have doubtless more than once asked, "Why are prayer and intercession not a greater joy and delight? Is there any way that we may be able to make fellowship with God our chief joy and, as intercessors, bring down His power and blessing on those for whom we pray?"

There may be more than one answer to the question, but the main one is undoubtedly that we know God too little. In our prayer, we do not seek His presence; it is not the main thing on which we set our hearts. And yet it should be so. We think mostly of ourselves, our need, our weakness, our desire and prayer.

We forget that in every prayer *God must be First, must be All*. To seek Him, to find Him, to wait in His presence, to be assured that *His holy presence rests upon us*, that He actually listens to what we say and is working in us — this alone is what makes prayer as natural and easy to us as the loving fellowship of a child with his father.

How is one to attain to this nearness to God and fellowship with Him? The answer is simple: *We must give God time to make Himself known to us*. Believe with your whole heart that just as you present yourself to God as a petitioner, so God presents Himself to you as the Hearer of prayer. But you cannot realize this until you give Him time and quiet. It is not the quantity or earnestness of your words that give prayer its power, but the living faith that *God Himself is taking you and your prayer into His loving heart*. He Himself will give the assurance that in His time your prayer will be heard.

Begin this day with the words, "To you, O Lord, I lift up my soul" (Ps. 25:1). Bow before Him in stillness, believing that He looks on you and will reveal His presence.

"My soul thirsts for God, for the living God" (Ps. 42:2).

Day 2

God Is a Spirit

"God is Spirit, and those who worship Him must worship in spirit and truth."
(John 4:24)

WHEN God created man and breathed into him of His own spirit, man became a living soul. The soul stood midway between the spirit and the body, and had to yield either to the spirit, to be lifted up to God, or yield to the flesh and its lusts. In the Fall, man refused to listen to the spirit and became the slave of the body. The spirit in man became utterly darkened.

In regeneration the spirit is quickened and born again from above. In the regenerate life of fellowship with God, the spirit of man always has to yield itself to the Spirit of God. The spirit is the deepest, most inward part of the human being. We read in Psalm 51:6, "You desire truth in the inward parts, and in the hidden part You will make me to know wisdom"; and in Jeremiah 31:33, "I will put My law in their minds, and write it on their hearts." Isaiah also says, "With my soul I have desired You in the night; yes, by my spirit within me I will seek You early" (26:9). The soul must sink down into the depths of the hidden spirit and call upon that to stir itself to seek God.

God is a Spirit, most holy and most glorious. He gave us a spirit so that we could have fellowship with Him. Through sin that power was darkened and nearly quenched. The only way to restore it is by presenting the soul in stillness before God to let His Holy Spirit work in our spirit. Deeper than our thoughts and feelings, God will in our inward part — in the spirit within us, if it has been regenerated — teach us to worship Him in spirit and in truth.

"The Father is seeking such to worship Him" (John 4:23). His Holy Spirit will teach us this if we wait on Him. Be still before God and yield your whole heart to believe in and to receive the gentle working of His Spirit. And breathe out such words as these: "My soul, be silent before God"; "With my soul I have desired You in the night; yes, with my spirit within me I will seek You early"; "On You, O God, I wait."

Day 3

Intercession and Adoration

Oh, worship the Lord in the beauty of holiness! (Psalm 96:9)

T HE better we know God the more wonderful becomes our insight into the power of intercession. We begin to understand that it is the great means by which man can take part in carrying out God's purpose. God has entrusted the whole of His redemption in Christ to His *people* — to make it known and to communicate its loveliness to men. In all this, intercession is the chief and essential element; it is how His servants enter into full fellowship with Christ and receive the power of the Spirit for service.

It is easy to see why God has so ordered it. God desires to renew us after His image and likeness, and the only way to do this is by making His desires our own, so that we breathe His disposition and in love sacrifice ourselves. Then we become, in a measure, like Christ, who "ever lives to make intercession" (Heb. 7:25). Such can be the life of the consecrated believer.

The clearer our insight into this great purpose of God, the more we will feel the need to enter into God's presence in a spirit of humble worship and holy adoration. When we take time to abide in God's presence and enter fully into His mind and will, our whole soul becomes possessed by the thought of His glorious purpose. This strengthens our faith that God will work out all the good pleasure of His will through our prayers. As the glory of God shines upon us and we realize how helpless we are, we rise to a level of faith that believes that God will do above all that we can ask or think (Eph. 3:20). Intercession leads us to see our need for deeper adoration, and adoration gives us new power for intercession. The two will be found to be inseparable.

The secret of true adoration can only be known by the soul that takes time to wait in God's presence — the soul that yields itself to God for Him to reveal Himself. Adoration prepares us for the great work of making God's glory known. "Oh, come, let us worship and bow down; let us kneel before the Lord our Maker. For He is our God. . . . Give to the Lord the glory due His name" (Ps. 95:6–7; 96:8).

Day 4

The Desire For God

With my soul I have desired You in the night. (Isaiah 26:9)

WHAT is the greatest and most glorious thing that man can find upon earth? It is nothing less than God Himself.

And what is the best and most glorious thing that a man needs to do every day? It is nothing less than to seek and know and love and praise this glorious God. As glorious as God is, so is the glory which begins to work in the heart and life of those who give themselves to God.

Have you learned this first and greatest thing you need to do every day — to seek this God, to meet Him, worship Him, live for Him and for His glory? It is a great step forward in the life of a Christian when he truly sees this and yields himself to consider fellowship with God every day as the chief end of his life.

Take time to ask yourself if this is not the truest, highest wisdom and the one purpose for which a Christian is above all to live — to know his God rightly, and to love Him with his whole heart. It is not only true, but God Himself strongly desires that you live this way with Him and, in answer to prayer, will enable you to do so.

Begin today. Take a word from God's Book to speak to Him in stillness of soul: "O God, You are my God; early will I seek You; my soul thirsts for You; my flesh longs for You . . . my soul follows close behind You. . . . With my whole heart I have sought You" (Ps. 63:1, 8; 119:10).

Repeat these words in deep reverence and childlike longing till their spirit and power enter your heart; and wait upon God till you begin to realize the blessedness of meeting with Him. As you persevere, you will learn to expect that holy fear and sense of God's presence to abide with you throughout the day.

"I waited patiently for the Lord; and He inclined to me, and heard my cry" (Ps. 40:1).

Day 5

Silent Adoration

Truly my soul silently waits for God. . . . My soul, wait silently for God alone,
for my expectation is from Him. (Psalm 62:1, 5)

WHEN man in his littleness and God in His glory meet, we all understand that what God says has infinitely more worth than what man says. And yet our prayers so often consist of our thoughts, of what we need, that we give God no time to speak to us. Our prayers are often so indefinite and vague. It is a great lesson to learn that to be silent before God is the secret of true adoration. Remember these promises: "In quietness and confidence shall be your strength" (Isa. 30:15); "I wait for the Lord, my soul waits, and in His word I do hope" (Ps. 130:5).

As the soul bows itself before Him, remembering His greatness, holiness, power and love, and seeking to give Him the honor, reverence and worship due Him, the heart will be open to sense the nearness of God and the working of His power.

Such worship of God — in which you bow low in your nothingness, and realize God's presence as He gives Himself to you in Christ Jesus — is the sure way to give Him the glory due Him; it leads to the highest blessedness to be found in prayer.

Do not imagine that it is time lost. Do not turn from it if at first it seems difficult or fruitless. Be assured that it brings you into a right relation to God. It opens the way to fellowship with Him. It leads to the blessed assurance that He is looking on you in tender love and working in you with a secret, divine power. As you become more accustomed to it, it will give you the sense of His presence abiding with you throughout the day. It will make you strong to testify for God. Someone has said, "No one is able to influence others for goodness and holiness beyond the amount that there is of God in him." People will begin to feel that you have been with God.

"The Lord is in His holy temple. Let all the earth keep silence before Him" (Hab. 2:20). "Be silent, all flesh, before the Lord, for He is aroused from His holy habitation!" (Zech. 2:13).

Day 6

The Light of God's Countenance

God is light. (1 John 1:5)
The Lord is my light. (Psalm 27:1)

EVERY morning the sun rises, and we walk in its light and perform our daily duties with gladness. Whether we think of it or not, the light of the sun shines on us all day.

Every morning the light of God shines on His children. But in order to enjoy the light of God's countenance, the soul must turn to God and trust Him to let His light shine in on it.

When there is a shipwreck at midnight, the sailors long for morning. How often the sigh goes up, "When will the day break?" In the same way, the Christian must wait on God patiently until His light shines on him. "My soul waits for the Lord more than those who watch for the morning" (Ps. 130:6).

Begin each day with one of these prayers: "Make Your face shine upon Your servant" (Ps. 31:16); "Lord, lift up the light of Your countenance upon us" (Ps. 4:6); "Cause Your face to shine, and we shall be saved!" (Ps. 80:3).

Do not rest until you know that the light of His countenance and His blessing is resting on you. Then you will experience the truth of the Scripture, "They walk, O Lord, in the light of Your countenance. In Your name they rejoice all day long" (Ps. 89:15–16).

The ardent longing of your Father is that you may dwell and rejoice in His light all day. Just as you need the light of the sun each hour, so the heavenly light, the light of the countenance of the Father, is indispensable. Just as we receive and enjoy the light of the sun, we can be confident that God desires to let His light shine on us.

Even when there are clouds, we still have the sun. Even in the midst of difficulties the light of God will rest on you without ceasing. If you are sure that the sun has risen, you count upon its light all the day. Make sure that the light of God shines upon you in the morning and you can count upon that light being with you all day long.

Do not rest until you have said, "Lord, lift up the light of Your countenance upon us." Take time till that light shines in your heart, and you can truly say, "The Lord is my light and my salvation" (Ps. 27:1).

Day 7

Faith In God

Jesus said to them, "Have faith in God." (Mark 11:22)

JUST as the eye is the organ by which we see light, so faith is the power by which we see the light of God and walk in it.

Man was made for God — made in His likeness; his whole being was formed after the divine pattern. Think of mankind's wonderful power of thinking out the thoughts of God hidden in nature. Think of the human heart, with its unlimited powers of self-sacrifice and love. Man was made for God, to seek Him, to find Him, to grow into His likeness and show forth His glory — in the fullest sense, to be His dwelling. And faith is the eye which, turning away from the world and self, looks up to God and in His light sees light. To faith God reveals Himself.

How often we try to awaken thoughts and feelings toward God which are but a faint shadow, and we forget to gaze on the Incomparable Original.

Could we but realize it, in the depth of our soul *God reveals Himself*!

Without faith it is impossible to please God or to know Him. In our quiet time we have to pray to our Father who is in the secret place. There He hides us in the secret place (see Psalm 27:5). And there, as we wait and worship before Him, He will — just as the light by its very nature reveals itself — let His light shine into our heart.

May our one desire be to take time and be still before God, believing with an unbounded faith in His longing to make Himself known to us. May we feed on God's Word, making us strong in faith. May that faith have large thoughts of God's glory, of His power to reveal Himself to us, of His longing to get complete possession of us.

Such faith, exercised and strengthened day by day in secret fellowship with God, will become the habit of our life, keeping us ever in the enjoyment of His presence and the experience of His saving power.

"Abraham was strong in faith, giving glory to God; being fully convinced that what He had promised He was also able to perform" (Rom. 4:20–21).

"I believe God, that it shall be just as it was told me" (Acts 27:25).

"Wait on the Lord; be of good courage, and He shall strengthen your heart. Wait, I say, on the Lord!" (Ps. 27:14).

Day 8

Alone With God

And it happened, as He was alone praying . . . (Luke 9:18)
He departed again to a mountain by Himself alone. (John 6:15)

MAN needs God. God made him for Himself, to find his life and happiness in Him alone. Man needs to be alone with God. His fall consisted of his being brought under the power of things visible and temporal through the lust of the flesh and the world. His restoration is meant to bring him back to the Father's house, to His presence, to His love and fellowship. Salvation means being brought to love and delight in the presence of God.

Man needs to be alone with God. Without this, God cannot have the opportunity to shine into his heart and transform his nature, to take possession of him and fill him with the fullness of God.

Man needs to be alone with God in order to yield himself to the presence and the power of His holiness and love. Christ could not live here on earth without at times separating Himself entirely from His surroundings and being alone with God. How much more must this be indispensable to us! When our Lord commanded us to enter our inner chamber, shut the door, and pray to our Father in secret, He promised us that the Father would hear such prayers and mightily answer them.

Alone with God — that is the secret of true prayer, of true power in prayer; of authentic, face-to-face fellowship with God, of power for service. There is no true, deep conversion, no real holiness, no clothing with the Holy Spirit and power, no abiding peace or joy, without a daily time alone with God. There is no path to holiness other than frequent and lengthy times alone with God.

What a privilege it is to begin every morning in daily secret prayer. May it be the one thing our hearts are set on.

Take time to be alone with God. Soon it will amaze you to hear someone suggest that five minutes could be enough. "Give heed to the voice of my cry, my King and my God, for to You I will pray. My voice You shall hear in the morning, O Lord; in the morning I will direct it to You, and I will look up" (Ps. 5:2–3).

Day 9

Wholly For God

Whom have I in heaven but You? And there is none upon earth that I desire besides You.
(Psalm 73:25)

ALONE with God — this is a word of the deepest importance. May we seek grace from God to reach its depths. Then we will learn another word of equally deep significance: wholly for God. If we find that it is not easy to persevere in being alone with God we will realize that it is because we are not wholly for God.

Because He is the only God, He alone has a right to demand that we be wholly for Him. Without this surrender He cannot make His power known. We read in the Old Testament that His servants Abraham, Moses, Elijah and David gave themselves wholly and unreservedly to God so that He could work out His plans through them. It is only the fully surrendered heart that can fully trust God for all He has promised.

If anyone desires to do a great work he must give himself wholly to it. This is especially true of a mother's care for her child. She gives herself wholly to the little one whom she loves. Is it not reasonable that the great God of Love should have us wholly for Himself? "Wholly for God" should be the keynote for our devotions every morning as we rise. As wholly as God gives Himself to us, so He desires that we give ourselves to Him.

Meditate on these things alone with God and ask Him by His almighty power to work in you all that is pleasing in His sight.

Wholly for God — what a privilege! What wonderful grace to fit us for it! Wholly for God means separation from men, and work, and all that might draw us away. Wholly for God leads to indescribable blessedness as the soul learns what it means and what God gives with it. "You shall love the Lord your God with all your heart, with all your soul, and with all your mind" (Matt. 22:37). "They . . . sought Him with all their soul; and He was found by them" (2 Chron. 15:15). "With my whole heart I have sought You" (Ps. 119:10).

Day 10

The Knowledge of God

"And this is eternal life, that they may know You." (John 17:3)

THE knowledge of God is absolutely necessary for the spiritual life; it is *life eternal.* I don't mean the intellectual knowledge we receive from others, but the living, experiential knowledge in which God makes Himself known to the soul. Just as the rays of the sun on a cold winter's day warm the body, so the living God sheds the life-giving rays of His holiness and love into the heart that waits on Him.

Why do we so seldom experience this life-giving power of the true knowledge of God? It is because we do not give God time to reveal Himself to us. When we pray, we think we know how to speak to God, but we forget that one of the first steps in prayer is to be silent before God, that He may reveal Himself. By His hidden but mighty power, God manifests His presence, resting on us and working in us. To know God in the personal experience of His presence is life indeed.

Brother Lawrence had a great longing to know God and for this purpose went into a monastery. His spiritual advisers gave him prayer books to use, but he put them aside. "It helps little to pray," he said, "if I do not know the God to whom I pray." He believed that God would reveal Himself. He remained a long time in silent adoration in order to become fully aware of the presence of this great and holy Being. He continued in this practice, until the day came when he lived consciously and constantly in God's presence, experiencing His blessed nearness and keeping power.

As the rising sun gives the promise of light throughout the day, so a quiet time of waiting on God, yielding ourselves to let Him shine on us, gives the promise of His presence and power resting on us all day. Be sure that the sun has risen on your soul.

As the sun on a cold day shines on us and imparts its warmth, the living God will work in us with His love and almighty power. God will reveal Himself as life and light and joy and strength to the soul that waits upon Him. "Lord, lift up the light of Your countenance upon us" (Ps. 4:6). "Be still, and know that I am God" (Ps. 46:10).

Day 11

God the Father

*"Make disciples . . . baptizing them in the name of the Father and of
the Son and of the Holy Spirit." (Matt. 28:19)*

THE doctrine of the Holy Trinity has a deep devotional aspect. As we think
of God the Father we remember the inconceivable distance that separates
Him in His holiness from sinful men, and we bow in deep contrition and holy
fear. As we think of Christ the Son we remember the inconceivable nearness
in which He came to be born of a woman, to die an accursed death, and so be
inseparably joined to us for all eternity. And as we think of the Holy Spirit we
remember the inconceivable blessedness of God having His abode in us and
making us His home and His temple through eternity.

When Christ taught us to say, "Our Father, which art in heaven," He immediately added, "hallowed be Thy name." As God is holy, so we are to be holy
too. And there is no way of becoming holy but by counting that name most
holy and drawing near to Him in prayer.

How often we speak that name — Father — without any sense of the
unspeakable privilege of our relation to God. If we would just take time to
come into contact with God and to worship Him in His Father love, the inner
chamber of our hearts would become to us the gate of heaven!

If you pray to your Father in secret, bow very low before Him and seek to
adore His name as most holy. Remember that this is the highest blessedness of
prayer. "Pray to your Father who is in the secret place; and your Father who
sees in secret will reward you openly" (Matt. 6:6).

What an unspeakable privilege, to be alone with God in secret and say, "My
Father" — to have the assurance that He has indeed seen me in that secret place
and will reward me openly. Take time in private prayer until you can say with
Jacob, "I have seen God face to face, and my life is preserved" (Gen. 32:30).

Day 12

God the Son

Grace to you and peace from God our Father and the Lord Jesus Christ.
(Rom. 1:7)

IT is remarkable that the Apostle Paul in each of his thirteen Epistles writes (with only minor variances), "Grace to you and peace from God our Father and the Lord Jesus Christ." He had such a deep sense of the inseparable oneness of the Father and the Son in the work of grace that in each opening benediction he refers to both.

This is a lesson for us of the utmost importance. There may be times in our Christian life when we think mostly of God the Father, and pray to Him. But later on we realize that it may cause spiritual loss if we do not grasp the truth that only through faith in Christ and in living union with Him can we enjoy a full and abiding fellowship with God.

In Revelation, John saw "a throne set in heaven, and One sat on the throne. . . . And the four living creatures . . . do not rest day or night, saying: 'Holy, holy, holy, Lord God Almighty, who was and is and is to come!'" (Rev. 4:2, 8).

Later he saw "in the midst of the throne . . . a Lamb as though it had been slain" (Rev. 5:6). No one in all the worshiping multitude could see God unless he first saw Christ the Lamb of God. And no one could see Christ without seeing the glory of God the Father and Son as inseparably One.

If you want to know and worship God rightly, seek Him and worship Him in Christ. And if you seek Christ, seek Him and worship Him in God. Then you will understand what it is to have your life "hidden with Christ in God" (Col. 3:3). Then you will experience the fellowship and adoration of Christ that is indispensable to the full knowledge of the love and holiness of God.

Be still, and speak these words in deepest reverence: "Grace and peace" — all I can desire — "from God the Father and the Lord Jesus Christ."

Take time to meditate, and then believe and expect all from God the Father who sits on the throne and from the Lord Jesus Christ, the Lamb in the midst of the throne. Then you will learn truly to worship God. Return frequently to this sacred scene, to give "glory . . . to Him who sits on the throne, and to the Lamb" (Rev. 5:13).

Day 13

God the Holy Spirit

Through Him we both have access by one Spirit to the Father. (Eph. 2:18)

IN our communion with God in the inner chamber of our hearts, we must guard against the danger of seeking to know God and Christ in the power of the intellect or the emotions. The Holy Spirit has been given for the express purpose that we may have access to the Father through the Son (Eph. 2:18). Let us be careful to wait for the teaching of the Spirit so that our labor is not in vain.

Christ taught His disciples this truth after their meal on the last night. Speaking of the soon coming of the Holy Spirit, He said, "Until now you have asked nothing in My name. Ask, and you will receive, that your joy may be full" (John 16:24). The Holy Spirit was given with the one great objective of teaching us to pray. He makes our fellowship with the Father and the Son a blessed reality. Be strong in faith that He is working secretly in you. As you enter the inner chamber, give yourself wholly to His guidance as your Teacher in all your intercession and adoration.

When Christ said to the disciples on the evening of the resurrection day, "Receive the Holy Spirit" (John 20:22), it was, for one thing, to strengthen and prepare them for the ten days of prayer that followed His ascension, and for their receiving the fullness of the Spirit. This suggests to us three things we ought to remember when we draw near to God in prayer:

1. We must pray in confidence that the Holy Spirit dwells in us, and yield ourselves, in stillness of soul, definitely to His leading. Take time for this.

2. We must believe that the "greater works" of the Spirit for the enlightening and strengthening of the spiritual life — the fullness of the Spirit — will be given in answer to prayer.

3. We must believe that through the Spirit, in unity with all God's children, we may ask for and expect the mighty workings of that Spirit on His Church and people.

"He who believes in Me, as the Scripture has said, out of his heart will flow rivers of living water" (John 7:38). Do you believe this?

Day 14

The Secret of the Lord

"Go into your room, and when you have shut your door, pray to your Father who is in the secret place; and your Father who sees in secret will reward you openly."
(Matt. 6:6)

CHRIST greatly longed for His disciples to know God as their Father and have secret fellowship with Him. In His own life He found it not only indispensable but the highest happiness to meet the Father in secret. And He wants us to realize that it is impossible to be true, wholehearted disciples without daily communion with the Father in heaven, who waits for us in the secret place of prayer.

God is a God who hides Himself from the world and all that is of the world. God wants to draw us away from the world and from ourselves. He offers us instead the blessedness of close, intimate communion with Himself. Oh, that God's children would understand this!

Believers in the Old Testament enjoyed this experience: "You are my hiding place" (Ps. 32:7); "He who dwells in the secret place of the Most High shall abide under the shadow of the Almighty" (Ps. 91:1); "The secret of the Lord is with those who fear Him" (Ps. 25:14).

Christians in the New Covenant ought to value this secret communion with God all the more. Paul tells us, "You are dead, and your life is hidden with Christ in God" (Col. 3:3). If we really believe this, we will have the joyful assurance that our life, hidden with Christ in God in such divine keeping, is safe and beyond the reach of every foe. We should confidently seek the renewal of our spiritual life through daily prayer to our Father who is in the secret place. Because we are dead with Christ, planted with Him in the likeness of His death and resurrection, we know that, as the roots of a tree are hidden under the earth, so the roots of our daily life are hidden deep in God.

Take the time to realize that God will hide you in the secret place of His presence (Ps. 31:20). Your first thought in prayer should be that you are alone with God, and that God is with you. "In the secret place of His tabernacle He shall hide me" (Ps. 27:5).

Day 15

Half an Hour Silence in Heaven

There was silence in heaven for about half an hour. Then another angel, having a golden censer, came and stood at the altar. And he was given much incense, that he should offer it with the prayers of all the saints upon the golden altar which was before the throne. (Rev. 8:1, 3)

THERE was silence in heaven for about half an hour to bring the prayers of the saints before God, before the first angel sounded his trumpet. And so ten thousands of God's children have felt the absolute need of silence and retirement from the things of earth for half an hour — to present their prayers before God and in fellowship with Him be strengthened for their daily work.

How often the complaint is heard that there is no time for prayer. And often the confession is made that, even if time could be found, one feels unable to spend it in real communion with God. We need not ask what prevents us from growing in our spiritual lives. The secret of strength can only be found in living communion with God.

Just obey Christ when He says, "When you have shut your door, pray to your Father who is in the secret place" (Matt. 6:6), and have the courage to be alone with God for half an hour. Do not worry that you won't know how to spend the time. Just begin and be faithful, and bow in silence before God, and He will reveal Himself to you.

If you need help, read a passage of Scripture, and let God's Word speak to you. Then bow in deepest humility before God, and wait on Him. *He will work within you.* Read Psalm 61, 62 or 63, and speak the words out before God. Then begin to pray. Intercede for your own household and children, for the congregation and minister, for schools and missions. Keep on, though the time may seem long. God will reward you. But above all, be sure you meet God.

God longs to bless you. Isn't it worth the trouble to take half an hour alone with God? In heaven itself there was need for half an hour's silence to present the prayers of the saints before God. If you persevere, you may find that the half-hour that seems the most difficult in the whole day may eventually become the most blessed in your whole life. "Truly my soul silently waits for God. . . . My soul, wait silently for God alone, for my expectation is from Him" (Ps. 62:1, 5).

Day 16

God's Greatness

For you are great, and do wondrous things; You alone are God.
(Psalm 86:10)

WHEN anyone begins an important work, he takes time to consider the greatness of his undertaking. Astronomers spend years of labor to grasp the magnitude of the heavenly bodies. Isn't our glorious God worthy of any time we take to know and adore His greatness?

Yet how superficial is our knowledge of God's greatness. We do not allow ourselves time to bow before Him and come under the deep impression of His incomprehensible majesty and glory. Meditate on the following texts until you are filled with some sense of what a glorious Being God is: "Great is the Lord, and greatly to be praised; and His greatness is unsearchable. . . . I will declare Your greatness. . . . They shall utter the memory of Your great goodness" (Ps. 145:3, 6, 7).

Do not imagine that it is easy to grasp the meaning of these words. Take time for them to master your heart, until you bow in speechless adoration before God. This is what Jeremiah did: "Ah, Lord God! . . . There is nothing too hard for You. . . . the Great, the Mighty God . . . great in counsel and mighty in work" (Jer. 32:17–19). And hear God's answer: "Behold, I am the Lord, the God of all flesh. Is there anything too hard for Me?" (32:27).

The right comprehension of God's greatness will take time. But if we give God the honor that is His due, and if our faith grows strong in the knowledge of what a great and powerful God we have, we will be motivated to spend time in the inner chamber of our hearts and bow in humble worship before this great and mighty God. In His abundant mercy He will teach us through the Holy Spirit to say, "The Lord is the great God, and the great King above all gods. . . . Oh come, let us worship and bow down; let us kneel before the Lord our Maker" (Ps. 95:3, 6).

Day 17

A Perfect Heart

For the eyes of the Lord run to and fro throughout the whole earth, to show Himself strong on behalf of those whose heart is loyal to [perfect toward, KJV] Him.
(2 Chron. 16:9)

IN worldly matters we know how important it is that work should be done with the whole heart. In the spiritual sphere this is likewise true. God has given the commandment, "You shall love the Lord your God with all your heart, with all your soul, and with all your might" (Deut. 6:5). And in Jeremiah 29:13 it says, "You will seek Me and find Me, when you search for Me with all your heart."

It is amazing that earnest Christians who tackle their daily work with all their hearts are so content to take things easy in the service of God. They do not seem to realize that, if anywhere, they should give themselves to God's service with all the power of their will.

The text above gives us an insight into the absolute necessity of seeking God with a perfect or loyal heart. What an encouragement this should be to us to humbly wait upon God with an upright heart; we can be assured that His eye is upon us, and He will show forth His mighty power in us and in our work.

Have you learned this lesson in your worship of God — to yield yourself each morning with your whole heart to do God's will? Pray each prayer with a perfect heart, in true wholehearted devotion to Him, and in faith expect the power of God to work in you and through you.

Remember that to come to this you must begin by being silent before God, until you realize that He is indeed working in the secret place of your heart. "I wait for my God" (Ps. 69:3). "In the secret place of His tabernacle He shall hide me" (Ps. 27:5).

Day 18

The Omnipotence of God

"I am Almighty God." (Gen. 17:1)

WHEN Abraham heard these words, he fell on his face, and God spoke to him, filling his heart with faith in what God would do for him. Have you bowed in deep humility before God until you sensed your living contact with the Almighty, until your heart was filled with faith that the mighty God is working in you and will perfect His work in you?

Read how the psalmists rejoiced in God and in His strength: "I will love You, O Lord, my strength" (18:1); "The Lord is the strength of my life" (27:1); "God is the strength of my heart" (73:26); "You . . . made me bold with strength in my soul" (138:3). Also look at such passages as Psalm 18:32, 46:1, 68:28, 68:35, 59:17 and 89:17. Take time to appropriate these words, and to adore God as the Almighty One, your strength.

Christ taught us that salvation is the work of God and quite impossible for man. When the disciples asked, "Who then can be saved?" His answer was, "With men this is impossible, but with God all things are possible." If we firmly believe this, we will also believe that God is working in us all that is pleasing in His sight.

Paul prayed for the Ephesians that through the enlightening of the Spirit they might know "the exceeding greatness of His power toward us who believe, according to the working of His mighty power" (1:19). And he prayed for the Colossians that they would be "strengthened with all might, according to His glorious power" (1:11). When we fully believe that the mighty power of God is working without ceasing within us, we can joyfully say, "God is the strength of my life."

Is it any wonder that many Christians complain of weakness and shortcomings? They do not understand that the Almighty God must work in them every hour of the day. That is the secret of the true life of faith. Do not rest until you can say to God, "I will love You, O Lord, my strength." Let God have complete possession of you and you will be able to say with all God's people, "You are the glory of their strength" (Ps. 89:17).

Day 19

The Fear of God

Blessed is the man who fears the Lord, who delights greatly in His commandments.
(Psalm 112:1)

THE fear of God — these words characterize the religion of the Old Testament and the foundation which it laid for the more abundant life of the New. The gift of holy fear is still the great desire of the child of God, and needs to be an essential part of any life that is to make a real impression on the world around it. It is one of the great promises of the new covenant in Jeremiah: "I will make an everlasting covenant with them . . . I will put My fear in their hearts so that they will not depart from Me" (32:40).

We find the perfect combination of two seeming opposites — fear and comfort — in Acts 9:31: "Then the churches . . . had peace and were edified. And walking in the fear of the Lord and in the comfort of the Holy Spirit, they were multiplied." Paul more than once gives fear a high place in the Christian life: "Work out your own salvation with fear and trembling; for it is God who works in you" (Phil. 2:12–13); ". . . perfecting holiness in the fear of God" (2 Cor. 7:1).

It has often been said that one of the ways in which our modern era does not compare favorably with the times of the Puritans and the Covenanters is our lack of the fear of God. No wonder, then, that there is a corresponding lack of the reading of God's Word, regular worshiping in His house, and the spirit of continuous prayer — all of which marked the early Church. It is essential that we preach on Scripture passages like those above and teach young believers about the need and the blessedness of a deep fear of God; this will lead to unceasing prayerfulness — one of the essential elements of the life of faith.

We must earnestly cultivate this grace in the inner chamber of our hearts, until we hear this word from heaven: "Who shall not fear You, O Lord, and glorify Your name? For You alone are holy" (Rev. 15:4). "Let us have grace, by which we may serve God acceptably with reverence and godly fear" (Heb. 12:28).

When we take the promise "Blessed is the man who fears the Lord" (Ps. 112:1) into our hearts and believe that it is one of the deepest secrets of blessedness, we will truly seek, every time we approach God, to worship Him in reverential fear. "Serve the Lord with fear, and rejoice with trembling" (Ps. 2:11).

Day 20

God Incomprehensible

"Behold, God is great, and we do not know Him. . . . As for the Almighty, we cannot find Him; He is excellent in power." (Job 36:26, 37:23)

THIS attribute of God as a Spirit whose being and glory are entirely beyond our power of apprehension is one that we ponder all too little. And yet in the spiritual life it is of utmost importance to be deeply aware that, as the heavens are high above the earth, so God's thoughts and ways are infinitely exalted beyond ours.

We must look to God with deep humility and holy reverence, and then with childlike simplicity, yield ourselves to the teaching of His Holy Spirit. "Oh, the depth of the riches both of the wisdom and knowledge of God! How unsearchable are His judgments and His ways past finding out!" (Rom. 11:33).

Let us respond in our hearts, "O Lord, how wonderful are all Your thoughts, and how deep are Your purposes." The study of God's attributes should fill us with holy awe and a sacred longing to know Him and honor Him properly.

Just think of His greatness — incomprehensible; His might — incomprehensible; His omnipresence — incomprehensible; His wisdom — incomprehensible; His holiness — incomprehensible; His mercy — incomprehensible; His love — incomprehensible.

As you worship, cry out, "What an inconceivable glory is in this Great Being who is my God and Father!" Then confess with shame how little you have sought to know Him properly, or to wait on Him to reveal Himself. Begin in faith to trust that, in a way passing all understanding, this incomprehensible and all-glorious God will work in your heart and life and grant you in ever-growing measure to know Him in truth. "My eyes are upon You, O God the Lord; in You I take refuge" (Ps. 141:8). "Be still, and know that I am God" (Ps. 46:10).

Day 21

The Holiness of God (O.T.)

"Be holy, for I am holy. . . . For I the Lord sanctify them." (Lev. 11:45, 21:23)

NINE times these phrases are repeated in Leviticus. Israel had to learn that as holiness is the highest and most glorious attribute of God, so it must be the marked characteristic of His people. Those who want to know God properly, and meet with Him in the secret place, must above all desire to be holy as He is holy. The priests who were to have access to God had to be set apart for a life of holiness.

It was the same for the prophets who spoke for Him. Isaiah said, "I saw the Lord sitting on a throne, high and lifted up. . . . And one [seraph] cried to another and said: 'Holy, holy, holy is the Lord of hosts . . .'" (6:1–3). This is the voice of adoration. "Then I said: 'Woe is me, for I am undone! . . . for my eyes have seen the King, the Lord of hosts'" (6:5). This is the voice of a broken, contrite heart. "Then one of the seraphim flew to me, having in his hand a live coal . . . from the altar. And he touched my mouth with it, and said: 'Behold . . . your iniquity is taken away, and your sin purged'" (6:6–7). This is the voice of grace and full redemption.

Then follows the voice of God: "Whom shall I send?" And the willing answer is, "Here am I! Send me" (6:8). Pause with holy fear and ask God to reveal Himself as the Holy One. "For thus says the High and Lofty One who inhabits eternity, whose name is Holy: 'I dwell in the high and holy place, with him who has a contrite and humble spirit'" (Isa. 57:15).

Be still, and take time to worship God in His great glory, and in His deep humility in which He longs and offers to dwell with us and in us. If you want to meet with your Father in the secret place, bow low and worship Him in the glory of His holiness. Give Him time to make Himself known to you. It is an unspeakable grace to know God as the Holy One. "You shall be holy, for I the Lord your God am holy" (Lev. 19:2); "Holy, holy, holy is the Lord of hosts" (Isa. 6:3); "Oh, worship the Lord in the beauty of holiness!" (Ps. 96:9); "And let the beauty of the Lord our God be upon us" (Ps. 90:17).

Day 22

The Holiness of God (N.T.)

"Holy Father, keep through Your name those whom You have given Me. . . . Sanctify them by Your truth. . . . And for their sakes I sanctify Myself, that they also may be sanctified by the truth." (John 17:11, 17, 19)

CHRIST forever lives to pray this great prayer. Expect and appropriate God's answer. Hear the words of Paul in First Thessalonians: "Night and day praying exceedingly . . . that He may establish your hearts blameless in holiness before our God. . . . Now may the God of peace Himself sanctify you completely. . . . He who calls you is faithful, who also will do it" (3:10, 13; 5:23–24).

Ponder deeply these words as you read them, and use them as a prayer to God: "Blessed Lord, strengthen my heart to be blameless in holiness. May God Himself sanctify me completely. I know God is faithful, who also will do it."

What a privilege to commune with God in secret, to speak these words in prayer, and to wait on Him until they live in our hearts through the working of the Spirit and we begin to know something of the holiness of God. "To the church of God which is at Corinth, to those who are sanctified in Christ Jesus, called to be saints" (1 Cor. 1:2). This is God's calling for you and me.

God's holiness has been clearly revealed in the Old Testament. In the New, we find the holiness of God's people in Christ, through the sanctification of the Spirit. May we understand the blessedness of saying, "Be holy, for I am holy" (Lev. 11:45). God is saying, "With you, O My children, as with Me, holiness should be the chief thing."

For this purpose the Holy, Holy, Holy One has revealed Himself to us, through the Son and the Holy Spirit. Let us use the word "holy" with great reverence of God, and then with holy desire for ourselves. Worship the God who says, "I am the Lord who sanctifies you" (Lev. 22:32). Bow before Him in holy fear and strong desire, and then, in the fullness of faith, listen to this prayer promise: "Now may the God of peace Himself sanctify you completely . . . who also will do it."

Day 23

Sin

And the grace of our Lord was exceedingly abundant, with faith and love which are in Christ Jesus . . . to save sinners, of whom I am chief. (1 Tim. 1:14–15)

NEVER forget for a moment, as you enter the secret place of prayer, that your whole relationship to God depends on what you think about sin and about yourself as a redeemed sinner. It is sin that makes God's holiness so glorious, because He has said, "Be holy, for . . . I am the Lord who sanctifies you" (Lev. 20:7–8).

It is sin that called forth the wonderful love of God in not sparing His Son. It was sin that nailed Jesus to the cross, and revealed the depth and the power of the love with which He loved. Through all eternity in the glory of heaven, it is our being redeemed sinners that will tune our praise.

Never for a moment forget that it is sin that has led to the great transaction between you and Christ Jesus; and that each day in your fellowship with God, His one aim is to deliver and keep you fully from its power and lift you up into His likeness and His infinite love.

It is the awareness of sin that will keep you low at His feet and give a deep undertone to all your adoration. It is the awareness of sin, always surrounding you and seeking to tempt you, that will give fervency to your prayers and urgency to the faith that hides itself in Christ. It is the awareness of sin that makes Christ so unspeakably precious, that keeps you every moment dependent on His grace, and gives you the ability to be more than a conqueror through Him who loved us. It is the awareness of sin that calls us to thank God with a broken and contrite heart which God will not despise, that works in us that contrite and humble spirit in which He delights to dwell.

It is in the inner chamber, in the secret place with the Father, that sin can be conquered, the holiness of Christ can be imparted, and the Spirit of holiness can take possession of our lives. In the inner chamber we learn to know and experience fully the divine power of these precious words of promise: "The blood of Jesus Christ His Son cleanses us from all sin. . . . Whoever abides in Him does not sin" (1 John 1:7, 3:6).

Day 24

The Mercy of God

Oh, give thanks to the Lord, for He is good! For His mercy endures forever.
(Psalm 136:1)

THIS psalm is wholly devoted to the praise of God's mercy. In each of the twenty-six verses we have the expression, "His mercy endures forever." The psalmist was full of this happy thought. Our hearts too should be filled with this blessed assurance. The everlasting, unchangeable mercy of God is cause for unceasing praise and thanksgiving!

Let us read now what is said about God's mercy in the well-known Psalm 103: "Bless the Lord, O my soul . . . who crowns you with lovingkindness and tender mercies" (v. 4). Of all God's communicable attributes, mercy is the crown. May it be a crown upon my head and in my life! "The Lord is merciful and gracious, slow to anger, and abounding in mercy" (v. 8).

Just as God's greatness is wonderful, so His mercy is infinite. "For as the heavens are high above the earth, so great is His mercy toward those who fear Him" (v. 11). What a thought! As high as the heaven is above the earth, so immeasurably and inconceivably great is the mercy of God, waiting to bestow His richest blessing. "The mercy of the Lord is from everlasting to everlasting on those who fear Him" (v. 17). Here again the psalmist speaks of God's boundless lovingkindness and mercy.

How frequently we read these familiar words without the least thought of their immeasurable greatness! Be still and meditate, until your heart responds as in the words of Psalm 36: "Your mercy, O Lord, is in the heavens" (v. 5). "How precious is Your lovingkindness, O God! Therefore the children of men put their trust under the shadow of Your wings" (v. 7). "Oh, continue Your lovingkindness to those who know You" (v. 10).

Take time to thank God with great joy for the wonderful mercy with which He crowns your life, and say, "Your lovingkindness is better than life" (Ps. 63:3).

Day 25

The Word of God

For the Word of God is living and powerful. (Heb. 4:12)

TO have communion with God, His Word and prayer are both indispensable; and in the inner chamber they should not be separated. In His Word, God speaks to me; in prayer, I speak to God.

The Word teaches me also to know the God to whom I pray; it teaches me how He wants me to pray. It gives me precious promises to encourage me in prayer. It often gives me wonderful answers to prayer. The Word comes from God's heart and brings His thoughts and His love into my heart. And then the Word goes back from my heart into His great heart of love, and prayer is the means of fellowship between God's heart and mine.

The Word teaches me God's will — the will of His promises as to what He will do for me (as food for my faith), and also the will of His commands, to which I surrender myself in loving obedience.

The more I pray, the more I feel my need of the Word and rejoice in it. The more I read God's Word, the more I have to pray about and the more power I have in prayer. One great cause of prayerlessness is that we read God's Word too little, or only superficially, or in the light of human wisdom.

It is the Holy Spirit through whom the Word has been spoken; He is also the Spirit of prayer. He will teach me how to receive the Word and how to approach God.

How blessed would the inner chamber be — what a power and an inspiration in our worship — if we only took God's Word as from Himself, turning it into prayer and definitely expecting an answer. In the inner chamber, in the secret of God's presence, God's Word becomes, through the Holy Spirit, our delight and our strength. God's Word — in deepest reverence in our hearts, on our lips, and in our lives — will be a never-failing fountain of strength and blessing.

Let us believe that God's Word is truly full of a quickening power to make us strong, enabling us to expect and receive great things from God. Above all, it gives us daily blessed fellowship with Him as the living God. "Blessed is the man . . . [whose] delight is in the law of the Lord, and in His law he meditates day and night" (Ps. 1:1–2).

Day 26

The Psalms

How sweet are Your words to my taste! Sweeter than honey to my mouth!
(Psalm 119:103)

OF the sixty-six books in the Bible, the Book of Psalms is given to us specifically to help us to worship God. The other books are historical, or doctrinal, or practical. But the psalms take us into the inner sanctuary of God's holy presence to enjoy the blessedness of fellowship with Him. It is a book of devotions inspired by the Holy Spirit. Do you want to truly meet God each morning, and worship Him in spirit and in truth? Then let your heart be filled with the Word of God through these psalms.

As you read the Book of Psalms, underline the word "Lord" or "God" wherever it occurs, and also the pronouns referring to God: "I," "You," "He." This will help to connect the contents of the psalm with God, who is the object of all prayer. When you have taken the trouble to mark the different names of God, you will find that more than one difficult psalm will have light shed upon it. These underlined words will make God the central thought and lead you to a new worship of Him. Take them on your lips and speak them out before Him. Your faith will be strengthened anew to realize how God is your strength and help in all circumstances of life.

Just as the Holy Spirit in ancient times used these psalms to teach God's people to pray, they can also teach us, by the power of that same Spirit, to abide continually in God's presence.

Take Psalm 119, for example. Every time that the word "God," "Lord," "You," or "Your" occurs, underline it. You will be surprised to find that each verse contains these words once or more than once. Meditate on the thought that the God who is found throughout this whole psalm is the same God who gives us His law and will enable us to keep it. This psalm will soon become one of your most beloved, and you will find its prayers and its teaching concerning God's Word drawing you continually up to God, in the blessed consciousness of His power and love. "Oh, how I love Your law! It is my meditation all the day" (Ps. 119:97).

Day 27

The Glory of God

To Him be glory . . . throughout all ages. (Eph. 3:21)

GOD Himself must reveal His glory to us; then alone are we able to know and glorify Him properly.

There is no more wonderful image of the glory of God in nature than the starry heavens. Telescopes, which are continually being made more powerful, have long proclaimed the wonders of God's universe. And through photography, new wonders of that glory have been revealed. If a photographic plate is fixed below a telescope, it can reveal millions of stars which cannot be seen by the eye through the best telescope. Man must step to one side and allow the glory of the heavens to reveal itself; then the stars, at first wholly invisible, and at immense distances, will leave their image upon the plate.

This is a lesson for those who long to see the glory of God in His Word. Put aside your own efforts and thoughts. Let your heart be as a photographic plate that waits for God's glory to be revealed. The plate must be rightly prepared and clean; let your heart be prepared and purified by God's Spirit. "Blessed are the pure in heart, for they shall see God" (Matt. 5:8). The plate must be immovable; let your heart be still before God. The plate must be exposed sometimes for seven or eight hours to receive the full impression of the farthest stars; let your heart take time in silent waiting upon God, and He will reveal His glory.

If you keep silent before God and give Him time, He will put thoughts into your heart that may be of unspeakable blessing to yourself and others. He will create within you desires and dispositions that will be like the rays of His glory shining in you.

Put this to the test this morning. Offer your spirit to Him in deep humility and have faith that God will reveal Himself in His holy love. His glory will descend upon you; you will feel the need to give Him adequate time to do His blessed work. "The Lord is in His holy temple. Let all the earth keep silence before Him" (Hab. 2:20). "My soul, wait silently for God alone, for my expectation is from Him" (Ps. 62:5). "God . . . has shone in our hearts to give the light of the knowledge of the glory of God in the face of Jesus Christ" (2 Cor. 4:6). "Be still, and know that I am God" (Ps. 46:10).

Day 28

The Holy Trinity

Elect according to the foreknowledge of God the Father, in sanctification of the Spirit, for obedience and sprinkling of the blood of Jesus Christ. (1 Peter 1:2)

HERE we have one of the texts in which the great truth of the blessed Trinity is seen to lie at the very root of our spiritual life. In our adoration of God the Father, we need sufficient time each day to worship Him in His glorious attributes. But we must remember that, in all our communion with God, the presence and the power of the Son and the Spirit are absolutely necessary.

What a field this opens for us in the inner chamber. We need to take time to realize how our communion with the Father is the result of the active and personal presence and working of the Lord Jesus. It takes time to become fully conscious of the need I have of Him in every time I approach God, the confidence I can have in the work that He is doing for me and in me, and how, in holy and intimate love, I may count on His presence and all-prevailing intercession. But to learn that lesson requires time — and that time will be most blessedly rewarded!

It is the same with the divine and almighty power of the Holy Spirit working in the depth of my heart — as the One who alone is able to reveal the Son within me. Through Him alone I have the power to know what and how to pray — especially how to plead the name of Jesus — and to receive the assurance that my prayer has been accepted.

Have you ever felt that it was a joke to speak of spending five minutes alone with God — as if that was all the time needed to sense His glory? Doesn't the thought of true worship of God in Christ through the Holy Spirit make you feel more than ever that it takes time to enter into such a holy alliance with God? By spending time in the secret of God's presence, you receive grace to abide in Christ and be led by His Spirit all day long.

Pause and think on this passage: "Elect according to the foreknowledge of God the Father, in sanctification of the Spirit, for obedience and sprinkling of the blood of Jesus Christ" (1 Pet. 1:2). What food for thought — and worship! "When You said, 'Seek My face,' my heart said to You, 'Your face, Lord, I will seek'" (Ps. 27:8).

Day 29

The Love of God

God is love, and he who abides in love abides in God, and God in him.
(1 John 4:16)

THE best and most wonderful word in heaven is love, for God is love. And the best and most wonderful word in the inner chamber of prayer must be love, for the God who meets us there is love.

What is love? It is the deep desire to give oneself for the beloved. Love finds its joy in imparting all that it has to make the loved one happy. And the heavenly Father, who offers to meet us in the inner chamber — let there be no doubt of this in our minds — has no other object than to fill our hearts with His love.

All the other attributes of God which have been mentioned find in this their highest glory. The true and full blessing of the inner chamber is nothing less than a life in the abundant love of God.

Because of this, our first and foremost thought in the inner chamber should be faith in the love of God. As you pray, seek to exercise great and unbounded faith in the love of God. Take time in silence to meditate on the wonderful revelation of God's love in Christ until you are filled with the spirit of worship and wonder and longing desire. Take time to believe the precious truth that "the love of God has been poured out in our hearts by the Holy Spirit who was given to us" (Rom. 5:5).

We should be ashamed at how little we have believed in and sought after God's love. As we pray, we should be confident that our heavenly Father longs to manifest His love to us, and be deeply convinced of the truth that He will and can do it. "Yes, I have loved you with an everlasting love" (Jer. 31:3). "That you, being rooted and grounded in love, may be able to comprehend with all saints what is the width and length and depth and height — to know the love of Christ which passes knowledge" (Eph. 3:17–19). "Behold what manner of love the Father has bestowed on us" (1 John 3:1).

Day 30

Waiting on God

On You I wait all the day. (Psalm 25:5)

IN the expression "waiting on God" we find a deep scriptural truth about the attitude of the soul in communion with God. Just think — as we wait on God, He may reveal Himself in us; He may teach us His will; He may do to us what He has promised, that in all things He may be the Infinite God.

In this attitude of soul we should begin each day. On awaking in the morning, in prayer and meditation, in our daily work, in striving after obedience and holiness, in struggling against sin and self-will — in everything we should wait on God, to receive what He will bestow, to see what He will do, to allow Him to be Almighty God.

Meditate on these precious promises of God's Word, and discover the secret of heavenly power and joy: "But those who wait on the Lord shall renew their strength; they shall mount up with wings like eagles" (Isa. 40:31). "Wait on the Lord; be of good courage, and He shall strengthen your heart; wait, I say, on the Lord" (Ps. 27:14). "Rest in the Lord, and wait patiently for Him" (Ps. 37:7).

The deep root of all scriptural theology is absolute dependence on God. As we practice this attitude, it will become more natural and blessedly possible to say, "On You I wait all the day." This is the secret of true, uninterrupted, silent adoration and worship.

Have you begun to learn the true worship of God? If so, the Lord's name be praised. Or have you only learned how little you know of it? For this, too, thank Him. If you long for a fuller experience of this blessing, seek Him for it, recognizing your absolute need, each day and all the day, to wait on God. May the God of all grace grant this. "I wait for the Lord, my soul waits, and in His word I do hope" (Ps. 130:5). "Rest in the Lord, and wait patiently for Him . . . and He shall give you the desires of your heart" (Ps. 37:7, 4).

Day 31

The Praise of God

For praise from the upright is beautiful. (Psalm 33:1)

PRAISE is always a part of adoration. Adoration, when it has entered God's presence, always leads to the praise of His name. Praise should be part of the incense we bring before God in our quiet time.

When the children of Israel crossed the Red Sea and were delivered from the power of Egypt, the joy of their redemption burst forth into a song of praise: "Who is like You, O Lord, among the gods? Who is like You, glorious in holiness, fearful in praises, doing wonders?" (Ex. 15:11).

In the Psalms we see what a large place praise ought to have in the spiritual life. There are more than sixty psalms of praise, and they occur more frequently as the book draws to its close. See Psalms 95–101, 103–107, 111–118, 134–138, 144–150. The last five are all "Hallelujah" (meaning "Praise the Lord") psalms, with the word appearing at the beginning and the end. And the very last repeats "praise Him" twice in every verse, and ends, "Let everything that has breath praise the Lord."

Let us take time to study this until our whole heart and life becomes one continual song of praise. "I will bless the Lord at all times; His praise shall continually be in my mouth" (Ps. 34:1). "Everyday I will bless You" (Ps. 145:2). "I will sing praise to my God while I have my being" (Ps. 146:2).

With the coming of Christ into the world there was a new outburst of praise in the song of the angels, the song of Mary, the song of Zacharias, and the song of Simeon. And then to find in the song of Moses and the Lamb the praise of God filling creation: "Great and marvelous are Your works, Lord God Almighty! . . . Who shall not fear You, O Lord, and glorify Your name? For You alone are holy" (Rev. 15:3–4). The final song of praise is in Rev. 19:1–6, with four shouts of "Alleluiah!" followed by "For the Lord God omnipotent reigns."

May your inner chamber of prayer and your quiet time with God always lead your heart to unceasing praise.

Month 3

The Secret of Intercession

Day 1

Intercession

Pray for one another. (James 5:16)

WHAT a glorious mystery there is in prayer! On the one hand, God in His holiness, love and power waits and longs to bless man; on the other, sinful man, a worm of the dust, brings down from God by prayer the very life and love of heaven to dwell in his heart.

But how much greater is the glory of intercession — when a person boldly tells God what he desires for others! He seeks to bring down on one soul, or even on hundreds or thousands, the power of eternal life with all its blessings.

Intercession is the holiest exercise of our boldness as God's children, the highest privilege and joy of our relationship with God. It is the power of being used by God as instruments for His great work of making men His dwelling place and showing forth His glory! The Church should count intercession as one of the chief means of grace, and seek above everything else to cultivate in God's children the power of an unceasing prayerfulness on behalf of the perishing world. When believers have been brought into this divine secret of intercession, they will feel the strength in unity of spirit and the assurance that God will certainly avenge His own elect who cry day and night to Him. When Christians stop looking for the solution in mere external union and instead aim at being bound together to the throne of God by an unceasing devotion to Jesus Christ and an unceasing prayer for the power of God's Spirit, the Church will put on her beautiful garments, will put on her strength, and will overcome the world.

OUR gracious Father, teach us the glory, blessing, and all-prevailing power of intercession. Give us the vision of what intercession means to Thee, as essential for carrying out Thy blessed purpose; what it means to ourselves as the exercise of our royal priesthood; and what it will mean to Thy Church, and to those dying in sin, in the bringing down of the Spirit in power — for Jesus' sake. Amen.

Day 2

The Opening of the Eyes

And Elisha prayed, and said, "Lord, I pray, open his eyes that he may see." . . . Elisha said, "Lord, open the eyes of these men, that they may see." (2 Kings 6:17, 20)

HOW wonderfully God answered Elisha's prayer for his servant! The young man saw the mountain full of fiery chariots and horsemen around Elisha, sent by God to protect His servant.

Elisha prayed again, and the Syrian army was blinded and led into Samaria. There Elisha prayed for the opening of their eyes, and they found themselves hopeless prisoners in the hand of the enemy.

We can pray Elijah's prayers today, by asking that our eyes may see God's wonderful provision for His Church in the baptism with the Holy Spirit. All the powers of heaven are available to us to serve in God's kingdom. How little the children of God live in the faith of that heavenly vision — the power of the Holy Spirit, on them, with them, and in them, giving them strength to witness joyfully for their Lord and His work!

But we need that second prayer too — that God may open the eyes of those of His children who do not as yet see the power which the world and sin have upon His people. They are as yet unconscious of the feebleness that marks the Church, making it impotent to do the work of winning souls for Christ and building up believers for a life of holiness and fruitfulness. Let us pray especially that God may open all eyes to see what the great and fundamental need of the Church is: intercessory prayer to bring down His blessing, that the unceasing power of the Spirit may be known.

OUR Father in heaven, Thou art so unspeakably willing to give us the Holy Spirit in power! Open our eyes, that we may realize fully the lowly state of Thy Church and people, and as fully what treasures of grace and power Thou art willing to bestow in answer to the fervent prayer of a united Church. Amen.

Day 3

Man's Place in God's Plan

*The heaven, even the heavens, are the Lord's; but the earth He has given
to the children of men. (Psalm 115:16)*

GOD created heaven as a dwelling for Himself — perfect, glorious, and most holy. He gave the earth to man as his dwelling — everything very good, but only as a beginning; it needed to be kept and cultivated. God had done the work; man was to continue and perfect it.

Think of the iron and coal hidden in the earth, and the steam hidden in water. It was left to man to discover and use all this, as we see in the network of railroads that span the world and the steamships that cover the ocean. God created all of it to be used this way, but its discovery and use was dependent on the wisdom and diligence of man. What the earth is today, with its cities and buildings, with its cornfields and orchards, it owes to man. God began and prepared the work to be carried out by man, in fulfillment of God's purpose. Nature teaches us the wonderful partnership to which God calls man for the carrying out of the work of creation to its destined end.

This law holds equally true in the kingdom of grace. In the gospel God has revealed the power of the heavenly life and the spiritual blessings that fill heaven. But He has entrusted to His people the work of making these blessings known, and making men partakers of them.

What diligence the children of this world show in seeking for the treasures that God has hidden in the earth for their use! Shall not the children of God be equally faithful in seeking for the treasures hidden in heaven, to bring them down in blessing on the world? It is by the unceasing intercession of God's people that His kingdom will come and His will be done on earth as it is in heaven.

EVER-BLESSED Lord, how wonderful is the place Thou hast given man, in trusting him to continue the work Thou hast begun. Open our hearts for the great thought that, through the preaching of the gospel and the work of intercession, Thy people are to work out Thy purpose. Lord, open our eyes — for Jesus' sake. Amen.

Day 4

Intercession in the Plan of Redemption

O You who hear prayer, to You all flesh will come. (Psalm 65:2)

WHEN God gave the world into the power of man, made in His own image, to be its ruler under Him, He planned that Adam would do everything with God and through God, and that God Himself would do all His work in the world through Adam. Adam was to be the owner, master, and ruler of the earth. When sin entered the world, Adam's power proved to be a terrible reality, for through him the earth and the whole race of man was brought under the curse of sin.

When God made the plan of redemption, His object was to restore man to the place from which he had fallen. God chose His servants from ancient times who, through the power of intercession, could ask what they wanted and it would be given to them. When Christ became man it was so that as man, both on earth and in heaven, He might intercede for man. And before He left the world, He imparted this right of intercession to His disciples. In the sevenfold promise of the Farewell Discourse (John 15–17), He declared that whatever they asked He would do for them.

God's intense longing to bless seems in some sense to be graciously limited by His dependence on the intercession that rises from the earth. He seeks to rouse the spirit of intercession that He may be able to bestow His blessing on mankind. God regards intercession as the highest expression of His people's readiness to receive and to yield themselves wholly to the working of His almighty power.

Christians need to realize that their true nobility and their only power with God is their right to pray, and expect God to hear prayer. It is only as God's children begin to see what intercession means to God's kingdom that they will realize how solemn their responsibility is.

Every believer needs to see that God waits for him to take his part. We need to know that the highest, the most blessed, the mightiest human fulfillment of the petition "as in heaven, so on earth," is the intercession that rises day and night, pleading with God for the power of heaven to be sent down into the hearts of men. May God burn into our hearts this one thought: Intercession in its omnipotent power is according to His will and is most certainly effective!

Day 5

God Seeks Intercessors

He saw that there was no man, and wondered that there was no intercessor.
(Isaiah 59:16)

FROM ancient times God has had intercessors among His people to whom He listened and through whom He gave deliverance. Here we read of a time of trouble when He sought for an intercessor in vain. And He wondered! Think of what that means — God was amazed that no one loved the people enough, or had sufficient faith in His power, to intercede on their behalf. If there had been an intercessor He would have given deliverance; without an intercessor His judgments came down (see Isaiah 64:7 and Ezekiel 22:30–31).

What an infinitely important place the intercessor holds in the kingdom of God! Is it not amazing that God should give men such power? And yet so few know what it is to take hold of His strength and pray down His blessing on the world.

When Christ ascended to heaven and took His place on the throne, He gave the work of the extension of His kingdom into the hands of men. Now the highest exercise of His royal power as Priest-King is prayer: "He ever lives to make intercession" (Hebrews 7:25). But all that Christ does in heaven is in fellowship with His people on earth. In divine humility, God wills that the working of His Spirit will follow the prayer of His people. He waits for their intercession because it shows how prepared their hearts are — how ready they are to yield to His Spirit's control.

God rules the world and His Church through the prayers of His people. That God should have made the extension of His kingdom to such a large extent dependent on the faithfulness of His people in prayer is a stupendous mystery and yet an absolute certainty. God calls for intercessors: in His grace He has made His work dependent on them; He waits for them.

OUR Father, open our eyes to see Thine invitation to us to play a part in extending Thy kingdom through faithful prayer and intercession. Give us such an insight into the glory of this holy calling that we may yield ourselves wholeheartedly to its blessed service. Amen.

Day 6

Christ as Intercessor

Therefore He is also able to save to the uttermost those who come to God through Him, since He ever lives to make intercession for them. (Heb. 7:25)

ISAIAH tells us that after God wondered that there was no intercessor, "His own arm brought salvation for Him. . . . The Redeemer will come to Zion" (59:16, 20). God Himself provided the true intercessor in Christ His Son: "And He bore the sin of many, and made intercession for the transgressors" (53:12).

In His life on earth Christ began His work as Intercessor. Think of the high-priestly prayer on behalf of His disciples and of all who should through them believe in His name. Think of His words to Peter: "I have prayed for you, that your faith should not fail" (Luke 22:32) — which proves how intensely personal His intercession is. And on the cross He spoke as Intercessor: "Father, forgive them."

Now seated at God's right hand, our great High Priest continues the work of unceasing intercession, with this difference: He gives His people power to take part in it. Seven times in His Farewell Discourse He repeated the assurance that what they asked He would do.

The power of heaven was at their disposal. The grace and power of God waited for man's bidding. Through the leading of the Holy Spirit they would know what the will of God was. They would learn in faith to pray in His name. He would present their petition to the Father, and through His and their united intercession the Church would be clothed with the power of the Spirit.

BLESSED Redeemer, what wonderful grace that Thou callest us to share in Thy intercession! Arouse in Thy redeemed people a consciousness of the glory of their calling, and the rich blessing which Thy Church in its impotence can, through intercession in Thy name, bring down on this earth. May Thy Holy Spirit deeply convict Thy people of the sin of prayerlessnes, of the laziness, unbelief, and selfishness that causes it, and of Thy loving desire to pour out the Spirit of prayer in answer to their petitions — for Thy name's sake. Amen.

Day 7

The Intercessors God Seeks

I have set watchmen on your walls, O Jerusalem, who shall never hold their peace day or night. You who make mention of the Lord, do not keep silent, and give Him no rest. (Isaiah 62:6–7)

WATCHMEN were placed on the walls of a city to warn of coming danger. God also appoints watchmen, not only to warn men — often they will not hear — but also to call for His aid whenever a need or enemy threatens. Intercessors are known for their persistence; they take no rest and give God no rest, until deliverance comes. In faith they may be assured that God will answer their prayer. This is what our Lord Jesus meant when He said, "Shall not God avenge His own elect who cry out day and night to Him?" (Luke 18:7).

The threat today is the influence of the world and the earthly-mindedness it brings. The Church is losing influence over its members. The evidence of God's presence, as seen in the conversion of sinners and the holiness of His people, is feeble at best. The great majority of Christians utterly neglect Christ's call to take part in extending His kingdom, and few experience the power of the Holy Spirit.

There is much discussion about how to spark interest in Bible study and awaken love for worship, but little talk of the indispensable necessity of the power of the Holy Spirit in the ministry and the membership of the Church. Few seem to know or admit that a lack of prayer is the reason that the workings of the Spirit are so feeble.

Only by united fervent prayer can a change be brought about. If ever there was a time when God's elect should cry day and night to Him, it is now. I urge you to offer yourself to God for this blessed work of intercession. Learn to count it the highest privilege of your life to be a channel through whose prayers God's blessing can be brought down to earth.

EVER-BLESSED Father, raise up intercessors, such as Thou wouldst have. Give us men and women to make mention of Thee, taking no rest and giving Thee no rest, until Thy Church again be a praise in the earth. Blessed Father, let Thy Spirit teach us how to pray. Amen.

Day 8

The School of Intercession

Who, in the days of His flesh . . . offered up prayers and supplications, with vehement cries and tears . . . and was heard because of His godly fear. (Heb. 5:7)

"CHRIST, the Head, is Intercessor in heaven; we, the members of His Body, are partners with Him on earth. Let no one imagine that it cost Christ nothing to become an intercessor. Were it not for His sacrifice, He could not be our example. Isaiah speaks three times of how He poured out His soul: "When You make His soul an offering for sin, He shall see His seed. . . . He shall see of the travail of His soul. . . . I will divide Him a portion with the great, because He poured out His soul unto death" (53:10–12).

The pouring out of the soul is the divine meaning of intercession. Nothing less than this was needed if His sacrifice and prayer were to have power with God. By giving of Himself to live and die that He might save the perishing, He reveals the kind of spirit that has power to prevail with God.

If we as helpers and fellow-laborers with the Lord Jesus are to share His power of intercession, we too need His travail of soul — the giving up of our life and its pleasures for the one supreme work of interceding for our fellow men. Intercession must not be a passing interest; it must become an ever-growing object of intense desire, which we long for above everything. It is the life of consecration and self-sacrifice that will indeed give power for intercession (Acts 15:26; 20:24; Phil. 2:17; Rev.12:11).

The longer we study this blessed truth and think of what it means to exercise this power for the glory of God and the salvation of men, the deeper will become our conviction that it is worth giving up everything to take part with Christ in His work of intercession.

BLESSED Lord Jesus, teach us how to unite with Thee in calling upon God for the souls Thou hast bought. Let Thy love fill us and all Thy saints, that we may learn to plead for the power of Thy Holy Spirit to be made known. Amen.

Day 9

The Name of Jesus the Power of Intercession

"Until now you have asked nothing in My name. In that day you will ask in My name;
ask and you will receive, that your joy may be full." (John 16:24, 26)

DURING Christ's life on earth the disciples had little knowledge of the power of prayer. In Gethsemane, Peter and the others utterly failed. They had no conception of what it was to ask in the name of Jesus and receive. The Lord promised them that in the days to come they would be able to pray with such power in His name that whatever they asked for would be given to them.

"Until now you have asked nothing," but "in that day you will ask in My name and will receive." These two conditions are still found in the Church. The great majority of Christians have such a lack of knowledge of their oneness with Christ, and of the Holy Spirit as the Spirit of prayer, that they do not even attempt to claim the wonderful promises Christ gives. But where God's children know what it is to abide in vital union with Christ, and to yield to the Holy Spirit's teaching, they begin to learn that their intercession is effective and that God gives the power of His Spirit in answer to their prayer.

It is faith in the power of Jesus' name, and our right to use it, that gives us the courage to follow on where God invites us to the holy office of intercessor. When our Lord Jesus gave His unlimited prayer promise, He sent the disciples out into the world with this conviction: "He who sits upon the throne, and who lives in my heart, has promised that what I ask in His name I shall receive. He will do it."

If Christians only knew what it is to yield themselves wholly and absolutely to Jesus Christ and His service, their eyes would be opened to see that intense and unceasing prayer is the essential mark of a healthy spiritual life. They would know that the power of all-prevailing intercession is for those who live only in and for their Lord!

BLESSED Savior, give us the grace of the Holy Spirit so to live in Thee, and with Thee, and for Thee, that we may boldly look to Thee for the assurance that our prayers are heard. Amen.

Day 10

Prayer the Work of the Spirit

God has sent forth the Spirit of His Son into your hearts, crying out, "Abba, Father."
(Gal. 4:6)

WE know what "Abba, Father" meant to Christ in Gethsemane. It was the entire surrender of Himself to death, to accomplish God's holy, loving plan to redeem sinners. In His prayer He was ready for any sacrifice, even giving up His life. That prayer reveals the heart of the One who sits at the right hand of God, the wonderful power of intercession that He exercises there, and His power to pour down the Holy Spirit.

The Holy Spirit is bestowed by the Father to breathe the very spirit of His Son into our hearts. Our Lord wants us to yield ourselves as wholly to God as He did — to pray like Him, that God's will of love should be done on earth at any cost. As God revealed His love in His desire to save us, so Jesus revealed His desire when He gave Himself for us. And He now asks His people to be filled with that same love and desire, and give themselves wholly to the work of intercession, praying down God's love upon the perishing.

To keep us from thinking this is beyond our reach, God gives the Holy Spirit to us so that we may actually pray as Jesus did, in His power and in His name. Whoever yields himself wholly to the leading of the Holy Spirit will feel compelled by divine love to a life of continual intercession, because he knows God is working in him.

Now we can understand how Christ could give such unlimited promises of answer to prayer to His disciples: they were first going to be filled with the Holy Spirit. Now we understand how God can give such a high place to intercession in the fulfillment of His purpose of redemption: it is the Holy Spirit who breathes God's own desire into us and enables us to intercede for souls.

ABBA, Father! Grant by Thy Holy Spirit that we may maintain an unceasing, loving intercession for those for whom Christ died. Give us a vision of the blessedness and power which come to those who yield themselves to this high calling. Amen.

Day 11

Christ Our Example in Intercession

And He shall divide the spoil with the strong, because . . . He bore the sin of many and made intercession for the transgressors. (Isaiah 53:12)

H E made intercession for the transgressors." Think of what it cost Him to pray that prayer effectively. He had to pour out His soul as an offering for sin and cry in Gethsemane: "Father, Thy holy, loving will be done."

What motivated Him to sacrifice Himself to the uttermost? It was His love for the Father — that His holiness might be manifest. It was His love for souls — that they might be partakers of His holiness.

Think of the reward He won! As Conqueror of every enemy He is seated at the right hand of God, with the power of unlimited, reliable intercession. And He will see His seed, a generation of those of the same mind as Him, whom He can train to share in His great work of intercession.

And what does this mean for us, when we seek to pray for the transgressors? We must also yield ourselves wholly to the Father and say, "Thy will be done, whatever it costs." We too must sacrifice ourselves, pouring out our soul unto death.

The Lord Jesus has taken us into partnership with Himself, to carry out the great work of intercession. He in heaven and we on earth must have one mind, one aim in life — that we should, out of love for the Father and for the lost, consecrate our lives to intercede for God's blessing. The burning desire of Father and Son for the salvation of souls must be the burning desire of our hearts, too.

What an honor! And what power for us to do the work. He lives and by His Spirit pours forth His love into our hearts!

EVERLASTING God of love, open our eyes to the vision of the glory of Thy Son, as He ever lives to pray. And open our eyes to the glory of that grace which enables us in His likeness also to live that we may pray for the transgressors, Father, for Jesus' sake. Amen.

Day 12

God's Will and Ours

"Your will be done." (Matt. 26:42)

GOD deserves to have everything in heaven and earth done according to His will. When He made man in His image it was, above all, that our desires be in perfect accord with the desires of God. This is the high honor of being in the likeness of God — that we can feel and wish just as God. In human flesh man was to be the embodiment and fulfillment of God's desires.

When God created man with the power to will and to choose, He limited Himself in the exercise of His will. And when man fell and yielded himself to the will of God's enemy, God in His infinite love set about the great work of winning man back to making the desires of God his own. In both God and man, desire is the great moving power. When man yielded himself to the things of the world, God sought to redeem him and teach him to live in harmony with Himself. His aim was to bring man's desire into perfect accord with His own.

The great step in this direction was when the Son of the Father came into this world to reproduce the divine desires in His own human nature, and in His life and through prayer yield Himself up continually to the perfect fulfillment of all that God wished and willed. The Son, as man, said in agony and blood, "Thy will be done," and surrendered even to being forsaken by God, that the power that had deceived man might be conquered and deliverance procured. It was in the wonderful and complete harmony between the Father and the Son — when the Son said, "Thy loving will be done" — that the great redemption was accomplished.

And now the great work of appropriating that redemption is this: that believers have to say first of all for themselves and then in lives devoted to intercession for others, "Thy will be done in heaven as on earth." As we plead for the Church — its ministers and missionaries, its strong Christians and young converts — and for the unsaved, whether nominally Christian or heathen, we have the privilege of knowing that we are pleading for what God wills and that through our prayers His will is to be done on earth as in heaven.

Day 13

The Blessedness of a Life of Intercession

You who make mention of the Lord, do not keep silent, and give Him no rest till He makes Jerusalem a praise in the earth. (Isaiah 62:6–7)

WHAT an unspeakable grace it is to be allowed to go to God in intercession for the needs of others!

What a blessing it is to take part in Christ's great work as Intercessor and to mingle my prayers with His! What an honor to have power with God in heaven over souls and to obtain for them what they do not know or think!

What a privilege, as stewards of the grace of God, to bring to Him the needs of groups or individuals, of local pastors or missionaries in faraway lands, and plead on their behalf till He entrusts us with the answer!

What blessedness, in union with other children of God, to strive together in prayer until the victory is gained over difficulties here on earth or over the powers of darkness in high places!

It is worth living for, to know that God uses us as intercessors to receive and dispense on earth His heavenly blessing and, above all, the power of His Holy Spirit.

This is the life of heaven, the life of the Lord Jesus Himself, in His self-denying love, taking possession of us and urging us to yield ourselves wholly to bear the burden of souls before Him and to plead that they may live.

For too long we have thought of prayer simply as a means of supplying our own needs in life and service. May God help us see the place intercession takes in His divine counsel and in His work for the kingdom. And may our hearts feel that there is no honor or blessedness on earth at all equal to the unspeakable privilege of waiting on God — bringing down from heaven and opening the way on earth for the blessing He delights to give!

FATHER, let Thy life flow down to earth and fill the hearts of Thy children! As the Lord Jesus pours out His love in unceasing intercession in heaven, so let it be with us on earth — a life of overflowing love and never-ending intercession. Amen.

Day 14

The Place of Prayer

These all continued with one accord in prayer and supplication. (Acts 1:14)

THE last words Christ spoke before He left earth give us the four great notes of His Church: "Wait for the Promise of the Father. . . . You shall receive power when the Holy Spirit has come upon you. . . . You shall be witnesses to Me . . . to the end of the earth" (Acts 1:4, 8).

United and unceasing prayer, the power of the Holy Spirit, living witnesses to the living Christ, to the end of the earth — such are the marks of the true gospel. Such is the ministry of the true Church of the New Testament — the Church that Christ founded, the Church that went out to conquer the world.

When Christ ascended to heaven, the disciples knew their job: to continue with one accord in prayer and supplication, being bound together by the love and Spirit of Christ into one Body. This is what gave them their wonderful power in heaven with God and on earth with men.

Their one duty was to wait in united and unceasing prayer for the power of the Holy Spirit, the endument from on high for their witness for Christ to the ends of the earth. A praying Church, a Spirit-filled Church, a witnessing Church, with all the world as its sphere and aim — such is the Church of Jesus Christ.

As long as the Church maintained this character it had power to conquer. But when it came under the influence of the world, how much it lost of its heavenly, supernatural beauty and strength! How unfaithful in prayer, how feeble the workings of the Spirit, how formal its witness to Christ, and how unfaithful to its worldwide mission!

BLESSED Lord Jesus, have mercy on Thy Church, and give the Spirit of prayer and supplication as of old, that Thy Church may prove what power from Thee rests upon her and her testimony for Thee, to win the world to Thy feet. Amen.

Day 15

Paul as an Intercessor

For this reason I bow my knees to the Father of our Lord Jesus Christ, that He would grant you . . . to be strengthened with might through His Spirit in the inner man.
(Eph. 3:14, 16)

WE think of Paul as a great missionary, preacher, and writer, as an apostle "in labors more abundant" (2 Cor. 11:23). But we do not often think of him as a great intercessor, who sought and obtained, by his supplication, the power that rested on all his other activities and brought down the blessing that rested on the churches he served.

In addition to the Ephesians (above), he prayed for the Thessalonians: "Night and day praying exceedingly, that we may see your face and perfect what is lacking in your faith . . . so that He may establish your hearts blameless in holiness" (1 Thess. 3:10, 13); the Romans: "Without ceasing I make mention of you always in my prayers" (1:9); the Philippians: "Always in every prayer of mine making request for you all with joy" (1:4); and the Colossians: "We . . . do not cease to pray for you. . . . For I want you to know what a great conflict I have for you" (1:9; 2:1).

Day and night he cried to God for them, for the light and power of the Holy Spirit to be in them; and as earnestly as he believed in the power of his intercession for them, he also believed in the blessing theirs would bring to him: "Now I beg you, brethren . . . that you strive together with me in your prayers to God for me" (Rom. 15:30); "God will yet deliver us, you also helping together in prayer for us" (2 Cor. 1:10–11); "Praying also for me, that I may open my mouth boldly" (Eph. 6:18–19; Col. 4:3; 2 Thess. 3:1); "This will turn out for my salvation through your prayer" (Phil. 1:19).

The whole relationship between pastor and people depends on united, continual prayer. Their whole relationship to each other is a heavenly one, spiritual and divine, and can only be maintained by unceasing prayer. When pastors and people wake up to the fact that the power and blessing of the Holy Spirit is waiting for their united and unceasing prayer, the Church will begin to know something of what apostolic Christianity is.

EVER-BLESSED Father, graciously restore again to Thy Church the spirit of supplication and intercession — for Jesus' sake. Amen.

Day 16

Intercession for Laborers

The harvest truly is plentiful, but the laborers are few. Therefore pray the Lord of the harvest to send out laborers into His harvest. (Matt. 9:37–38)

THE disciples understood little of what these words meant. Christ gave them as a seed-thought, to be lodged in their hearts for later use. At Pentecost, when they saw many of the new converts ready to testify for Christ in the power of the Spirit, they must have felt how the ten days of continuous united prayer had brought this blessing too, as the fruit of the Spirit's power — laborers in the harvest.

Christ meant to teach us that however large the field may be, and however few the laborers, prayer is the best, the sure, the only means for supplying the need.

We must understand that it is not only in time of need that we should pray; the whole work is to be carried out in the spirit of prayer. Prayer for laborers is in perfect harmony with our whole life and effort.

When China Inland Mission had grown to 200 missionaries, they held a conference in China. They felt there was such a deep need in unreached districts that, after much prayer, they asked God for 100 additional laborers and £10,000 for expenses, within the next year. They agreed to continue in prayer daily throughout the year. At the end of the time 100 suitable men and women had been found, with £11,000.

The churches see the needy world, its open fields and waiting souls, and complain about the lack of laborers and funds. Doesn't Christ call us to the united and unceasing prayer of the first disciples? God is faithful, by the power of His Spirit, to supply every need. Let the Church take a stand in united prayer and supplication. God hears prayer.

BLESSED Lord Jesus, teach Thy Church what it means to live and labor for Thee in the Spirit of unceasing prayer, that our faith may rise to the assurance that Thou wilt, in a way surpassing all expectation, meet the crying need of a dying world. Amen.

Day 17

Intercession for Individuals

And you will be gathered one by one, O you children of Israel. (Isaiah 27:12)

EVERY member in our body has its appointed place. It is the same in society and in the Church. The work must always aim at the welfare and highest perfection of the whole, through the cooperation of every individual member.

Too often the Church takes the attitude that the salvation of men is the work of the pastor. However, he generally deals only with the crowd and seldom reaches the individual. This is the cause of a twofold evil. First, the individual believer flounders because he does not understand that witnessing to those around him not only reaches lost people, but it nourishes and strengthens his own spiritual life as well. Second, unbelievers suffer unspeakable loss because Christ is not personally brought to them by each believer they meet.

Seldom do many Christians think of interceding for those around them. If this practice were restored to its rightful place in the Christian life, think what it would mean to the Church and to missions! When will Christians learn the great truth that what God desires to do in heaven is dependent upon prayer on earth? As we realize this, we discover that intercession is the chief element in the conversion of souls. All our efforts are in vain without the power of the Holy Spirit, given in answer to prayer. When pastors and people unite in a covenant of prayer and testimony, the Church will flourish. Oh, that every believer might understand the part he has to take!

As you begin to get an insight into the need and power of intercession, start exercising it on behalf of individuals. Pray for your children, relatives and friends, for all with whom God brings you into contact. If you feel you lack the power to intercede, let this truth humble you and drive you to the mercy seat: God wants every redeemed child of His to intercede for the perishing. It is the vital breath of the normal Christian life — the proof that one is born from above.

Also, pray intensely and persistently that God will bestow the power of His Holy Spirit on you and His children around you. Then the power of intercession will have the place that God can honor.

Day 18

Intercession for Pastors

And for me. (Eph. 6:19)
Praying also for us. (Col. 4:3)
Finally, brethren, pray for us. (2 Thess. 3:1)

THESE requests by Paul suggest the strength of his conviction that the Christians had power with God, and that their prayer was sure to bring new strength to him in his work. Because he sensed the actual unity of the Body of Christ and the interdependence of each member, humble or honorable, on the life that flowed through the whole Body, he sought to rouse Christians, for their sake and for his, and especially for the sake of the kingdom of God, with this call: "Continue earnestly in prayer, being vigilant in it with thanksgiving; meanwhile praying also for us" (Col. 4:2–3).

The Church depends on the ministry to an extent that we hardly realize. The place of the pastor is so high — a steward of the mysteries of God and an ambassador for God who pleads with men in Christ's name to be reconciled to Him — that unfaithfulness or inefficiency brings a terrible blight on the Church he serves. If Paul, having preached for twenty years in the power of God, still needed the prayer of the Church, how much more do pastors in our day need it?

The pastor needs the prayer of his people. He has a right to it, and he is truly dependent on it. It is his task to train Christians for their work of intercession on behalf of the Church and the world. He must begin by training them to pray for him. And he may need to begin still farther back and learn personally to pray more for himself and for them.

Let all intercessors who are seeking to enter more deeply into their blessed work give a larger place to the pastors in their own church and other churches. Let them plead with God for individuals and group ministries. Let them continue in prayer for pastors to be men of power, of prayer, and full of the Holy Spirit. Pray for the ministry!

OUR Father in heaven, arouse believers to a sense of their calling to pray for the ministers of the gospel in the spirit of faith. Amen.

Day 19

Prayer for All the Saints

Praying always with all prayer and supplication in the Spirit, being watchful to this end with all perseverance and supplication for all the saints. (Eph. 6:18)

NOTICE how Paul repeats words in his intense desire to reach the hearts of his readers: "Praying always with all prayer and supplication . . . with all perseverance and supplication." It is all prayer, all seasons, all perseverance, all supplication. These words deserve our attention if they are to bring about the necessary response in us.

Paul so deeply desired the unity of the Body of Christ, and was so sure that this unity could be realized only through love and prayer, that he pleaded with the believers at Ephesus to pray unceasingly and fervently for all saints — not only those in their immediate circle but all those they heard about. Unity is strength. As we exercise this power of intercession with all perseverance, we will be delivered from self with all its feeble prayers and given a larger heart, in which the love of Christ can flow freely and fully through us.

The great lack in true believers often is that their prayers are for themselves and what God must do for them. We need to realize that every believer is called to give himself without ceasing to the exercise of love and prayer. It is as we forget ourselves, trusting that God will take care of us, and yield ourselves to the great and blessed work of calling down the blessing of God on our brothers and sisters, that the whole Church is fit to do its work in making Christ known to every creature. This alone is the healthy and blessed life of a child of God who has yielded himself wholly to Christ Jesus.

Pray for God's children and the Church around you. Pray for all the work in which they are, or ought to be, engaged. Pray at all seasons in the Spirit for all God's saints. There is no blessedness greater than that of abiding communion with God. And there is no way that leads to the enjoyment of this more surely than the life of intercession for which these words of Paul appeal so pleadingly.

Day 20

Missionary Intercession

Then, having fasted and prayed, and laid hands on them, they sent them away.
(Acts 13:3)

HOW to multiply the number of Christians who will individually and collectively wield the force of intercession for the conversion and transformation of men is the supreme question of foreign missions. Every other consideration and plan is secondary to that of wielding the forces of prayer.

I take it for granted that those who love world missions will follow the scriptural injunction to pray unceasingly for its triumph. In morning devotions, in prayer services, in all times and seasons they will have an attitude of intercession that refuses to let God go until He crowns His workers with victory.

Missions have their root in the love of Christ, which was proved on the cross and now lives in our hearts. Just as men are so earnest in carrying out God's plans for the natural world, so God's children should be at least as wholehearted in bringing Christ's love to all mankind. Intercession is the chief means appointed by God to bring redemption within the reach of all.

Pray for missionaries, that the Christ-life in them may be clear and strong; that they may be men of prayer and filled with love, and the power of their spiritual life be evident.

Pray for national Christians, that they may know the glorious mystery among the nations: Christ in them, the hope of glory.

Pray for discipleship classes and students in schools, that the teaching of God's Word may be in power. Pray especially for national pastors and evangelists, that the Holy Spirit may fill them to be witnesses for Christ among their fellow countrymen.

Pray, above all, that the Church of Christ may be lifted out of its indifference and that every believer's objective in life will be to help to make Christ King on the earth.

OUR gracious God, our eyes are on Thee. In mercy hear our prayer, and by the Holy Spirit reveal the presence and the power of Christ in the work of Thy servants. Amen.

Day 21

The Grace of Intercession

Continue earnestly in prayer, being vigilant in it with thanksgiving;
meanwhile praying also for us. (Col. 4:2–3)

NOTHING can bring us nearer to God, nor lead us deeper into His love, than the work of intercession. Nothing can give us a higher experience of the likeness of God than the power of pouring out our hearts into the bosom of God in prayer for those around us. Nothing can so closely link us to Jesus Christ, the great Intercessor, nor give us the experience of His power and Spirit resting on us, as giving our lives to the work of bringing redemption to the hearts of our fellow men.

In nothing will we know more of the powerful working of the Holy Spirit than in the prayer breathed by Him into our hearts, "Abba, Father" — in all the fullness of meaning that it had for Christ in Gethsemane. Nothing can so help us prove the power and the faithfulness of God to His Word as when we reach out in intercession to the multitudes, either in the Church of Christ or in the world. As we pour out our souls as a living sacrifice before God, with the one persistent plea that He will, in answer to our prayer, open the windows of heaven and send down His abundant blessing, God will be glorified, our souls will reach their highest destiny, and God's kingdom will come.

Nothing will so help us understand and experience the living unity of the Body of Christ, and the irresistible power that it can exert, as the daily and continued fellowship with God's children in the persistent plea that God will arise and have mercy upon Zion and make her a light and a life to those who are sitting in darkness. How little we realize what we are losing in not living in fervent intercession! Think what we could gain for ourselves and for the world if we allow God's Spirit of grace and supplication to master our whole being!

In heaven Christ lives to pray; His whole intercourse with His Father is prayer — asking and receiving the fullness of the Spirit for His people. God delights in nothing so much as in prayer. Shall we not learn to believe that the highest blessings of heaven will be unfolded to us as we pray more?

BLESSED Father, pour down the Spirit of supplication and intercession on Thy people — for Jesus Christ's sake. Amen.

Day 22

United Intercession

There is one Body and one Spirit. (Eph. 4:4)

OUR own bodies teach us how essential it is for health and strength that every member seek the welfare of the whole. It is the same in the Body of Christ, but sadly, too many think of salvation only in terms of their own happiness. Many believers know that they do not live for themselves and truly seek in prayer and work to bring others to share in their happiness; but even many of them do not yet understand that, in addition to their personal circle or church, they have a calling to enlarge their hearts to take the whole Body of Christ into their love and intercession.

This is what the Spirit and the love of Christ will enable them to do. It is only when intercession for the whole Church, by the whole Church, ascends to God's throne, that the Spirit of unity and power can have its full sway.

The desire for closer union between different branches of the Church of Christ is cause for thanksgiving. But the difficulties, especially internationally, are so great that the thought of a united Church on earth appears beyond reach. But, thank God, the unity in Christ Jesus is deeper and stronger than any visible expression of it.

And there is a practical way that the Church, even in all its diversity, can demonstrate its unity, while strengthening and blessing the work of the kingdom. By cultivating the life of the Spirit and practicing intercession, this true unity can be realized. As believers learn the meaning of their calling as a royal priesthood, they will be led to see that God is not confined in His love or promises to their limited spheres of labor. He invites them to enlarge their hearts and, like Christ and the apostle Paul, to pray for all who believe or will come to believe. Then this earth and the Church of Christ in it will by intercession be bound to the throne of heaven as never before.

Let Christians and pastors bind themselves together for this worldwide intercession. It will strengthen their confidence that prayer will be heard, and that their prayers, too, will become indispensable for the coming of the kingdom.

Day 23

Unceasing Intercession

Pray without ceasing. (1 Thess. 5:17)

HOW different is the average Christian's concept of life in the service of God from that which Scripture gives us! Many believers think of the Christian life mainly in terms of their personal safety: they receive pardon for sin and the promise of heaven. High above this is the Bible standard: a Christian surrenders all of himself — his time, his thoughts, his love — to the glorious God who redeemed him, whom he now delights in serving, and in whose fellowship heaven has begun.

To most believers the command "Pray without ceasing" is a needless and impossible life of perfection. Who can do it? Can't we get to heaven without it? To the true believer, it promises the highest happiness — a life crowned by all the blessings that can be brought to others through his intercession. And as he perseveres, it becomes increasingly his highest aim on earth, his greatest joy, his deepest experience of fellowship with the holy God.

"Pray without ceasing!" Let us receive that word with great faith, as a promise of what God's Spirit will work in us — of how close and intimate our union to the Lord Jesus can be, and our likeness to Him, in His ever-blessed intercession at the right hand of God. Let it become one of the main elements of our heavenly calling as vessels of God's grace to the world around us.

Christ said, "I in them, and You in Me" (John 17:23); just as the Father worked in Him, so Christ, the interceding High Priest, will work and pray in us. As the faith of our high calling fills our hearts, we will begin to see that nothing on earth can compare with the privilege of being God's priests, of walking continuously in His holy presence, of bringing the burden of those around us to the throne, and receiving at His hands the power and blessing to dispense to our fellow men. This is the fulfillment of our creation in the image and likeness of God.

Day 24

Intercession Links Heaven with Earth

Your will be done on earth as it is in heaven. (Luke 11:2)

WHEN God created heaven and earth, He meant heaven to be the divine pattern to which earth was to conform. "As in heaven, so on earth" was to be the law of its existence.

The glory of heaven is that God is all in all there: everything lives in Him and for His glory. But think of what this earth has become, in all its sin and misery: the vast majority of humans lack any knowledge of the true God and most of the rest are nominal Christians — utterly indifferent to His call on their lives and estranged from His holiness and love. What is needed is a revolution, a miracle, if the word "As in heaven, so on earth" is to be fulfilled.

How is this ever to come true? Through the prayers of God's children! Our Lord teaches us to pray for it. Intercession is to be the great link between heaven and earth. The intercession of the Son, begun upon earth, continued in heaven, and carried on by His redeemed people upon earth, will bring about the mighty change: "As in heaven, so on earth." Christ said, "I delight to do Your will, O my God" (Psalm 40:8), and ultimately prayed the great prayer in Gethsemane, "Your will be done." Now His redeemed ones, who yield themselves fully to His mind and Spirit, can make His prayer their own and unceasingly send up the cry, "Your will be done, as in heaven, so on earth."

Every prayer of a parent for a child, of a believer for the lost, or for more grace to the saved, is part of the great unceasing cry going up day and night: "As in heaven, so on earth."

When God's children learn to pray not only for their immediate circles and interests, but enlarge their hearts to take in the whole Church and the whole world, their united supplication will have power with God and hasten the day when it shall indeed be "as in heaven so on earthî — the whole earth filled with the glory of God. Child of God, will you not yield yourself, like Christ, to live with this one prayer: "Father, Your will be done on earth as in heaven"?

OUR Father in heaven, hallowed be Thy name. Thy kingdom come, Thy will be done — as in heaven, so on earth. Amen.

Day 25

The Fulfillment of God's Desires

For the Lord has chosen Zion; He has desired it for His habitation: "This is my resting place forever; Here I will dwell, for I have desired it." (Psalm 132:13–14)

HERE is the one great desire of God that moved Him in the work of redemption: the longing of His heart for man — to dwell with him and in him.

To Moses He said: "Let them make Me a sanctuary; that I may dwell among them." And just as Israel had to prepare the dwelling for God, His children are now called both to yield themselves as a dwelling for God and to win others to become His habitation. As God's desire for us fills our hearts, it will awaken within us the desire for others to become His dwelling too.

What an honor! What a high calling, to count my worldly business as entirely secondary and to find my life and my delight in winning souls in whom God may find His heart's delight! "Here I will dwell, for I have desired it."

Through intercession, I can pray for God to give His Holy Spirit to those around me. It is God's great plan that man himself shall build Him a habitation. In answer to the unceasing intercession of His children, God will give His power and blessing. As this great desire of God fills us, we will give ourselves wholly to labor for its fulfillment.

Consider David's response to God's desire to dwell in Israel: "I will not give sleep to my eyes or slumber to my eyelids, until I find a place for the Lord, a dwelling place for the mighty God of Jacob" (Psalm 132:4–5). And shall not we, who know what that indwelling of God is, give our lives to fulfill His heart's desire?

Let us begin, as never before, to pray for our loved ones, for others around us, and for all the world — not only because we love them, but because God longs for them and gives us the honor of being the channels through whom His blessing is brought down. Wake up to the realization that God seeks to train you as intercessors, through whom the great desire of His loving heart can be satisfied!

O GOD, who hast said of human hearts, "Here I will dwell, for I have desired it," teach us to pray, day and night, that the desire of Thy heart may be fulfilled. Amen.

Day 26

The Fulfillment of Man's Desire

Delight yourself also in the Lord, and He shall give you the desires of your heart.
(Psalm 37:4)

GOD is love, an ever-flowing fountain, out of which streams an unceasing desire for His creatures to share in all His holiness and blessedness. The desire for the salvation of souls is God's perfect will, His highest glory.

This loving desire of God, to take His place in the hearts of men, is given to all His children who are willing to yield themselves wholly to Him. The likeness and image of God consist of having a heart in which His love takes complete possession and leads us to find spontaneously our highest joy in loving as He does.

It is thus that our text finds its fulfillment: "Delight yourself also in the Lord," and in His life of love, "and He shall give you the desires of your heart." The intercession of love, rising up to heaven, will be met with the fulfillment of the desires of your heart. We may be sure that, as we delight in what God delights in, such prayer is inspired by God and will have its answer. And our prayer becomes unceasingly, "Your desires, Father, are mine. Your holy, loving will is my will, too."

In fellowship with Him we receive the courage to bring those we care about before His throne, with an ever-growing confidence that our prayer will be heard. As we reach out in yearning love, we have the power to take hold of the will of God to bless, and to believe that God will work out His own blessed will in giving us the desires of our hearts — because the fulfillment of His desire is the delight of our souls.

We then become, in the highest sense of the word, God's fellow laborers. Our prayer becomes part of God's divine work of reaching and saving the lost. And we learn to find our happiness in losing ourselves in the salvation of those around us.

OUR Father, teach us that nothing less than delighting ourselves in Thee, and in Thy desires toward men, can inspire us to pray properly and give us the assurance of an answer. Amen.

Day 27

My Great Desire

One thing I have desired of the Lord, that will I seek: that I may dwell in the house of the Lord all the days of my life, to behold the beauty of the Lord, and to inquire in His temple. (Psalm 27:4)

HERE we have man's response to God's desire to dwell in us. When the desire of God toward us begins to rule the life and heart, our desire is fixed on one thing: to dwell in the house of the Lord all the days of our life, to behold the beauty of the Lord, to worship Him in the beauty of holiness. Then we may inquire in His temple and learn what God meant when He said, "I, the Lord, have spoken it, and I will do it. . . . I will also let the house of Israel inquire of Me to do this for them" (Ezekiel 36:36–37).

The more we realize God's loving desire to give His rest in our hearts and the more our desire grows to dwell every day in His temple and behold His beauty, the more the Spirit of intercession will grow in us, so that we want to claim all that God has promised in His new covenant. Whatever our concerns may be — our church and country, our home and school, our nearer or wider circle, the saved and their needs or the unsaved and their danger — the thought that God is indeed longing to find His home and His rest in the hearts of men, to be "inquired of," will rouse our whole being to strive for Zion's sake to pray. All thoughts of our feebleness and unworthiness will be swallowed up in the wonderful assurance that He has said of human hearts, "This is my resting place forever; here will I dwell, for I have desired it" (Psalm 132:14).

As we see how high our calling is, and how indispensable God has made fervent, intense, persistent prayer to fulfilling His purposes, we will be drawn to give up our life to gain a closer walk with God, an unceasing waiting upon Him, and a testimony to others of what God can do in one's life.

Is it not wonderful beyond all thought, this divine partnership in which God commits the fulfillment of His desires to our keeping? Shame on us that we have so little realized it!

OUR Father in heaven, give the Spirit of grace and supplication, in power, to Thy people — for Jesus' sake. Amen.

Day 28

Intercession Day and Night

"And shall God not avenge His own elect who cry out day and night to Him,
though He bears long with them?" (Luke 18:7)

WHEN Nehemiah heard of the destruction of Jerusalem, he cried to God, "Hear the prayer of Your servant which I pray before You now, day and night" (1:6). Of the watchmen set on the walls of Jerusalem, God said, "Who shall never hold their peace day or night" (Isaiah 62:6). And Paul writes, "Night and day praying exceedingly . . . so that He may establish your hearts blameless in holiness before our God and Father" (1 Thess. 3:10, 13).

Is such prayer night and day really needed and really possible? Of course, if the heart is so supremely possessed by the desire that it cannot rest until it is fulfilled. If your life is completely under the power of the heavenly blessing, nothing can keep you from sacrificing all to obtain it.

When a child of God begins to get a real vision of the needs of the Church and the world, of God's divine redemption in the outpouring of His love into our hearts, of the power of true intercession to bring down the heavenly blessing, and of the honor of being allowed to take part in that work, it comes as a matter of course that he regards intercession as the most heavenly thing upon earth — to cry day and night to God for the revelation of His mighty power.

Let us learn from David, who said, "Zeal for Your house has eaten me up" (Psalm 69:9), and from Christ our Lord, of whom these words were so intensely true. Let us learn that there is nothing more worth living for than satisfying the heart of God in His longing for human fellowship and affection, and winning hearts to be His dwelling place. And should we not also strive to find a place for the Mighty One in our hearts, and give our lives for the great work of intercession?

God grant that our hearts may be so influenced by these divine truths that our main goal in life will be devotion to Christ and satisfying the heart of God.

LORD Jesus, the great and glorious Intercessor, breathe Thine own Spirit into our hearts — for Thy name's sake. Amen.

Day 29

The High Priest and His Intercession

Therefore He [Jesus Christ, our High Priest] is also able to save to the uttermost those who come to God through Him, since He ever lives to make intercession for them.
(Heb. 7:25–26; 8:1)

THERE was a great difference between the high priest of Israel and the priests and Levites. The high priest alone had access to the Holiest of All. He bore on his forehead the golden crown engraved with "Holiness to the Lord," and by his intercession on the great Day of Atonement he bore the sins of the people. The priests brought the daily sacrifices, stood before the Lord, and came out to bless the people. The difference between high priest and priest was great. But still greater was the unity; they formed one body with the high priest, sharing with him the power to appear before God to receive and dispense His blessing to His people.

It is the same with our great High Priest. He alone has power with God, in a never-ceasing intercession, to obtain from the Father what His people need. And yet, though the distance is infinite between Him and the royal priesthood that surrounds Him for His service, the unity and fellowship which His people have with Him is no less infinite. He holds the blessing He obtained from His Father for us, waiting for us to receive it from Him through fervent supplication, and expecting us, in turn, to dispense it to those He has placed us among as His witnesses and representatives.

As long as Christians think only of being saved and of living in a way which will make that salvation secure, they never can understand the mysterious power of intercession to which they are called.

But salvation means a vital life-union with Jesus Christ — an actual sharing of His life, with Him dwelling and working in us. It is the consecration of our whole being to live and labor, to think and will, and to find our highest joy in living as a royal priesthood. When believers realize this, the Church will put on her strength and prove, in her relationships with God and men, how truly the likeness and power of Christ dwell in her.

O GOD, open our hearts to know and prove what our royal priesthood is: what the real meaning is of our living and praying in the name of Jesus, so that what we ask shall indeed be given to us! O Lord Jesus, our holy High Priest, breathe the spirit of Thine own holy priesthood into our hearts. Amen.

Day 30

A Royal Priesthood

Call to Me, and I will answer you, and show you great and mighty things,
which you do not know. (Jer. 33:3)

AS you plead for the great mercies of the new covenant to be bestowed, take with you these thoughts:

1. God is infinitely willing to bless. His very nature proves it: He delights in mercy; He waits to be gracious; His promises and the experience of His saints assure us of it.

2. Why then does the blessing so often tarry? Because, in creating man with a free will and making him a partner in the rule of the earth, God limited Himself. He made Himself dependent on what man would do. Man by his prayer holds the measure of what God can do in blessing.

3. Think of how God is hindered and disappointed when His children do not pray, or pray but little. The low, feeble life of the Church, the lack of the power of the Holy Spirit for conversion and holiness, is all owing to the lack of prayer. How different would be the state of the Church and the world if God's people were to take no rest in calling upon Him!

4. And yet God has blessed, just up to the measure of the faith and the zeal of His people. We should not be content with this as a sign of His approval. Instead, we should ask ourselves, If He has blessed our feeble efforts and prayers, what will He do if we yield ourselves completely to a life of intercession?

5. Our lack of consecration has kept back God's blessing from the world. What a call this is to repentance! He was ready to save men, but we were not willing to sacrifice with wholehearted devotion to Christ and His service.

God counts upon you to take your place before His throne as an intercessor. Wake up to the reality of your holy calling as a member of a royal priesthood. Begin to live in the assurance that intercession, in both the likeness to and the fellowship with the interceding Lord Jesus in heaven, is the highest privilege you can desire. In this spirit, take up this promise with large expectations: "Call to Me, and I will answer you, and show you great and mighty things, which you do not know."

Are you willing to give yourself wholly to this blessed calling? In the power of Jesus Christ, will you make interceding for God's Church and people, and for a dying world, the main goal of your life? Is this asking too much? Is it too much to give your life to this holy service of the royal priesthood, for the sake of that blessed Lord who gave Himself for us?

Day 31

Intercession a Divine Reality

Then another angel, having a golden censer, came . . . and he was given much incense,
that he should offer it with the prayers of all the saints upon the
golden altar which was before the throne. (Rev. 8:3)

IS it fair to suggest, as I have, that the Church has given a far too subordinate place to intercession in its teaching and practice? Is it not of such supreme importance that it is an essential, altogether indispensable element in the true Christian life? To those who take God's Word in its full meaning, there can be no doubt about the answer.

Intercession is, by amazing grace, an essential element in God's redeeming purpose — so much so that without it failure may lie at our door. Christ's intercession in heaven is essential to His carrying out the work He began upon earth. But to attain His goals, He also calls for the intercession of the saints. Just think of what we read: "All things are of God, who has reconciled us to Himself by Jesus Christ, and has given us the ministry of reconciliation" (2 Cor. 5:18). Just as the reconciliation was dependent on Christ's doing His part, to accomplish the work He calls on the Church to do her part. We see how Paul regarded intercession day and night as indispensable to the fulfillment of the work that had been entrusted to him. It is but one aspect of that mighty power of God which works in the heart of His believing people.

Intercession is indeed a divine reality. Without it, the Church loses one of its chief beauties — the joy and the power of the Spirit-life for achieving great things for God. Without it, the command to preach the gospel to every creature can never be carried out. Without it, there is no power for the Church to recover from her sickly, feeble life and conquer the world. And in the life of the believer, lay or clergy, there can be no entrance into the abundant life and joy of daily fellowship with God unless he takes his place among God's select — the watchmen of God who cry to Him day and night.

Church of Christ, wake up! Listen to the call: "Pray without ceasing. Take no rest, and give God no rest." Let your answer be, even though it be with a sigh from the depths of the heart, "For Zion's sake will I not hold my peace." God's Spirit will reveal to us the power of a life of intercession as a divine reality, an essential and indispensable element of the great redemption, and therefore also of the true Christian life.

May God help us to know and fulfill our calling!

Month 4

The Secret of United Prayer

Day 1

The Lost Secret

He commanded them . . . to wait for the promise of the Father. . . .
"You shall be baptized with the Holy Spirit not many days from now." (Acts 1:4–5)

AFTER our Lord had given the great command, "Go into all the world and preach the gospel to every creature" (Mark 16:15), He added another, His very last: "Tarry . . . until you are endued with power from on high" (Luke 24:49). And He elaborated, ". . . you shall be baptized with the Holy Spirit not many days from now."

All Christians agree that the great command to preach the gospel was not only for the disciples but for us too. But many do not appear to consider that the very last command — not to preach until they had received power from on high — is also for us. We appear to have lost what ought to be our greatest secret — that only by living daily in the power of the Holy Spirit can we preach the gospel in power.

This is why there is so much preaching and working with so little spiritual result, and why there is so little consistent prayer — especially the kind of prayer that brings down power from on high.

The secret of Pentecost is found in the words and the deeds of our blessed Master — and His disciples, as they took Him at His word and continued with one accord in prayer until the promise was fulfilled. They then became full of the Holy Spirit and proved what the mighty power of their God could do through them.

Only the Holy Spirit can reveal to us what no eye has seen, nor ear heard, nor has entered into the heart of man — the things which God loves to do for those who wait upon Him (1 Cor. 2:9). Let us pray that the lost secret may be found — the sure promise that in answer to fervent prayer the power of the Holy Spirit will indeed be given.

Day 2

The Kingdom of God

Jesus presented Himself alive to His apostles, being seen by them during forty days and speaking of the things pertaining to the kingdom of God. (Acts 1:3)

WHEN Christ began to preach He took up the message of John: "The kingdom of heaven is at hand" (Matt. 4:17). Later He declared that "some standing here . . . will not taste death till they see the kingdom of God present with power" (Mark 9:1). Only after the King had ascended to His throne were His disciples ready to receive the Holy Spirit, bringing the heavenly power of the kingdom into their hearts.

Acts 1:3 says that the kingdom of God summed up all the teaching of Jesus during the forty days after the Resurrection; and likewise do the closing verses of Acts, describing Paul's teaching at Rome: "He . . . testified of the kingdom of God, . . . preaching the kingdom of God" (Acts 28:23, 31).

Christ, enthroned as King and Lord of all, entrusted to His disciples the news of the kingdom. The prayer He taught them, "Your kingdom come" (Matt. 6:10), now had a new meaning. The rule of God in heaven came down in the power of the Spirit, filling the disciples with one ambition: to proclaim the coming of the Spirit into the hearts of men. The kingdom of God was now on earth, a kingdom ruling and dwelling with men, as in heaven.

Our Lord's last command to His disciples (Acts 1:4–8) included six essential elements of the kingdom: 1) the King — the crucified Christ; 2) the disciples — His faithful followers; 3) their power for service — the Holy Spirit; 4) their work — testifying for Christ as His witnesses; 5) their goal — the ends of the earth; 6) their first duty — waiting on God in united, unceasing prayer.

If we are to continue the prayer of the disciples, we need to understand what Christ told them, and what it meant for their inner life and outward service.

Day 3

Christ Is King

And He said to them, "Assuredly, I say to you that there are some standing here
who will not taste death till they see the kingdom of God present with power."
(Mark 9:1)

THE first mark of the Church is that Christ is King. When Christ said that the kingdom would come in power within the lifetime of some who heard Him, He meant that when He, as King, had ascended to the throne of the Father, the kingdom would be revealed in the hearts of His disciples by the power of the Holy Spirit. In heaven, God's will is always being done; in the power of the Holy Spirit, Christ's disciples do His will even as it was done in heaven.

The nature of a kingdom is seen in its King. Christ reigns as God and man on His Father's throne. On earth the kingdom is invisible; its power is seen only in the lives of those in whom it rules. Only in the Church, the members of Christ, is the united Body seen and known; Christ lives and rules in their hearts. Our Lord Himself taught how close the relationship would be: "At that day you will know that I am in My Father, and you in Me, and I in you" (John 14:20). Next to their faith in His oneness with God and their trust in His omnipotent power was the knowledge that they lived in Him and He in them.

Here is our first lesson if we are to follow in the steps of the disciples and share their blessing: we must know that Christ as King actually dwells and rules in our hearts. We must know that we live in Him and that in His power we are able to accomplish all He would have us do. Our whole life is to be devoted to our King and the service of His kingdom.

This blessed relationship to Christ will mean, above all, a daily fellowship with Him in prayer. The prayer life is to be a continuous and unbroken exercise. In this way His people can rejoice in their King and in Him can be more than conquerors.

Day 4

Jesus the Crucified

"God has made this Jesus, whom you crucified, both Lord and Christ."
(Acts 2:36)

CHRIST is our Lord and King. But one fact must not be overlooked: This King is none other than the crucified Jesus. All that we have to say about Him — His divine power, His abiding presence, His wonderful love — does not teach us to know Him properly unless we maintain a deep awareness that our King is the crucified Jesus. God has placed Him in the midst of His throne as a Lamb, looking as if it had been slain, and it is in this form that the hosts of heaven adore Him. It is the slain Lamb that we worship as King.

Christ's cross is His highest glory. Through the cross He has conquered every enemy and gained His place on the throne of God. And He must impart this condition of death to us too, if we are to know the full meaning of victory over sin. When Paul wrote, "I have been crucified with Christ . . . Christ lives in me" (Gal. 2:20), he taught us that it was as the crucified One that Christ ruled on the throne of his heart, and that the spirit of the cross should triumph over us as it did in him.

This was true of the disciples. This was their deepest preparation for receiving the Holy Spirit; they had, with their Lord, been crucified to the world. The old man had been crucified; in Him they were dead to sin and their life was hidden with Christ in God. Each one of us needs to experience this fellowship with Christ in His cross if the Spirit of Pentecost is really to take possession of us. It was through the Eternal Spirit that Christ gave Himself as a sacrifice and became the King on the throne of God. As we become "conformed to His death" (Phil. 3:10) — in the entire surrender of our will, the entire self-denial of our old nature, and the entire separation from the spirit of this world — we become the worthy servants of a crucified King and our hearts the worthy temples of His glory.

Day 5

The Apostles

And being assembled together with them, He commanded them not to depart from Jerusalem, but to wait for the Promise of the Father. (Acts 1:4)

IF we want a correct understanding of the outpouring of the Spirit in answer to the prayer of the disciples, we must answer this question: What prepared these men for such powerful, effective prayer and the wonderful fulfillment of the promise that came to them?

They were simple, unlearned men with many faults, whom the Lord had called to forsake all and follow Him. They had done this, as far as they could; they followed Him in the life He led and the work He did. Though they were still quite sinful, and powerless to fully deny themselves, their hearts clung to Him in deep sincerity. In the midst of much stumbling they still followed Him to the cross. They shared with Him His death; they died with Him to sin and were raised with Him in the power of a new life. This prepared them to have power in prayer and to be clothed with the power from on high.

Let this be the test by which we measure ourselves: Have we surrendered to the fellowship of Christ's sufferings and death? Have we hated our own life and crucified it and received the power of Christ's life in us? This will give us liberty to believe that God will hear our prayer too, and give us His Holy Spirit to work in us what we and He desire — if we are indeed with one accord to take up the disciples' prayer and to share in the answer. We must, like them, be willing learners in the school of Jesus and seek above everything that intimate fellowship with Him which will prepare us to pray the prayer of Pentecost and receive its answer.

Day 6

Not of This World

"They are not of the world, just as I am not of the world." (John 17:14, 16)

ON the night before He was crucified, our Lord made clear to His disciples the impassable gulf between Him and the world — and likewise between them and the world (John 17:6–21). He said of the Spirit, "The world cannot receive [Him], because it neither sees Him nor knows Him" (John 14:17). And of them: "Because you are not of the world . . . the world hates you" (John 15:19).

After Pentecost one great mark of the disciples was that they sought to be as little of the world as Christ was of the world. They became united with Christ in the cross and the resurrection; they belonged to another world, the kingdom of heaven. Separation from the world must be the mark of all disciples who long to be filled with the Spirit.

Why is faith in the Holy Spirit so little preached and practiced in the church? The world rules too much in the life of Christians. Christians so often fail to live out their calling to a heavenly life in Christ Jesus. First John 2:15–16 defines the love of the world as "the lust of the flesh" (pleasure in eating and drinking, in ease and comfort), "the lust of the eyes" (delight in all that the world offers of beauty and possession), and "the pride of life" (self-exaltation in what the wisdom and power of man has accomplished). All this robs the heart of its susceptibility and desire for that true self-denial that fits a person for receiving the Holy Spirit.

Anyone who seeks for the power of the Holy Spirit should ask himself if the spirit of the world is not the reason he lacks a love for prayer, which is absolutely necessary for those who plead for the promise of the Father. May the Lord write this deep in every heart: The world cannot receive the Holy Spirit! "You are not of the world, just as I am not of the world."

Day 7

Obedience

"If you love Me, keep My commandments. And I will pray the Father, and He will give you another Helper." (John 14:15–16)

WHEN the disciples began their training for the baptism of the Spirit, they needed to continue "with one accord" in prayer for the power of the Spirit. Christ was everything to them — even before the cross, but much more after His death and resurrection. He was literally their life, their one thought, their only desire.

Was such devotion to Christ something special and not to be expected of every believer? Or is it really what the Lord asks of all who desire to be filled with the Spirit? God expects it of all His children. The Lord needs people like this now as much as He did in the past, to receive His Spirit and His power, to minister His grace on earth, and, as intercessors, to link the world to the throne of God.

Is Christ *nothing, something,* or *everything* to us? For the unconverted, Christ is nothing; for the half-converted — the average Christian — Christ is something; for the true Christian, Christ is all. Each one who prays for the power of the Spirit must be ready to say, "I yield myself with my whole heart this day to the leading of the Spirit." A full surrender becomes a question of life or death, an absolute necessity.

The attitude of surrender — to live every day, all the day, abiding in Christ and keeping His commandments — is to be the one mark of your discipleship. It is only when your heart longs in everything to do God's will that the Father's love and Spirit can rest upon you. This was the disposition in which the disciples continued with one accord in prayer. This will be the secret of power in our intercession as we plead for the Church and the world.

Day 8

The Holy Spirit

"You shall be baptized with the Holy Spirit. . . .
You shall receive power when the Holy Spirit has come upon you." (Acts 1:5, 8)

ONE mark of the Church is power for service through the Holy Spirit. Since the time of Adam's fall — when he lost the spirit God had breathed into him — God's Spirit had struggled with men and worked in some with power, but He had never been able to find His permanent home in them.

It was only after Christ came, to break the power of sin by His death and give us new life by His resurrection, that the Spirit of God could take possession of the human heart and make it a dwelling for God.

Nothing less than this is the power in the disciples — and in us — by which sin can be overcome and prisoners set free. This Spirit is the Holy Spirit. In the Old Testament He was called the Spirit of God. But now the holiness of God is revealed in the cross of Christ, and through His cross Christ sanctifies us that we might be set apart like Him. On the Day of Pentecost the Spirit of God's holiness descended to dwell in men and take possession of them as God's holy temple.

He is also the Spirit of the Son. On earth He led the Son first into the desert to be tempted by Satan, then to the synagogue in Nazareth to proclaim Himself as the fulfillment of what the prophets had spoken (Isa. 61:1; Luke 4:18).

And so daily, all the way to the cross, Christ yielded Himself implicitly to the leading of the Spirit.

The Spirit now reveals Christ in us as our life and our strength, so that we may walk in perfect obedience and preach the Word in the power of God.

This is the amazing mystery: the Spirit of God is our life, and the Spirit of Christ is our light and strength. Only as we are led by the same Spirit who guided the first disciples will we have the power to pray the effective, fervent prayer of the righteous man that avails much.

Day 9

The Power from on High

"Tarry in the city of Jerusalem until you are endued with power from on high."
(Luke 24:49)

THE Lord told the disciples, "Without Me you can do nothing" (John 15:5). Why, then, did He choose these impotent, helpless men and send them out to conquer the world for Him? He did it so that in their feebleness they might yield themselves to Him and give Him, as Lord, the opportunity to show His power working through them. As the Father had done all the work in Christ when He was upon earth, so Christ in heaven would now be the Great Worker, proving in them that all power had been given to Him in heaven and on earth. Their place would be to pray, to believe, and to yield themselves to the mighty power of Christ.

The Holy Spirit would not be in them as a power *they* possessed; He would possess *them*, and their work would be the work of the Almighty Christ. They would live each day in unceasing dependence and prayer, and in confident expectation.

The apostles knew Christ intimately. They witnessed His mighty works, received His teaching, and walked with Him through all His sufferings, even to His death on the cross. They not only saw Him but knew Him in the power of His resurrection; they experienced that resurrection life in their own hearts. Yet they were incapable of truly making Him known until He Himself, from the throne of heaven, had taken possession of them by His Spirit *dwelling* in them.

The gospel minister must be content with nothing less than the indwelling life and power of the Holy Spirit. It is the only thing that can make us fit to preach the gospel in power. Nothing less than Christ speaking through us in the power of His omnipotence will make us able ministers of the New Testament, bringing salvation to those who hear us.

Day 10

My Witnesses

"You shall be witnesses to Me." (Acts 1:8)

CHRIST'S servants are to be witnesses for Him — testifying of His wonderful love, His power to redeem, His continual abiding presence, and His power to work in them.

This is the only weapon that the King allows His redeemed ones to use. Without claiming authority or power, without wisdom or eloquence, without influence or position, each one is called, not only by his words but by his life and action, to be a living witness to and proof of what Jesus can do.

This is the only weapon they are allowed to use to conquer men and bring them to the feet of Christ. This is what the first disciples did. When they were filled with the Spirit they began to speak of the mighty things that Christ had done.

In this power, those who were scattered abroad by persecution went as far as Antioch, preaching in the name of Jesus — and a multitude believed. They had no commission from the apostles, and no special gifts or training — but out of the fullness of their heart they spoke of Jesus Christ! They could not be silent; they were filled with the life and love of Christ and had to *witness* for Him. This is what caused the gospel to increase: every new convert became a witness for Christ.

A secular writer later said that if the Christians had been content to keep the worship of Jesus to themselves they would not have had to suffer persecution. But in their zeal they wanted Christ to rule over all.

The secret to a flourishing Church is for every believer to be a witness for Jesus. The reason for the weakness of the Church is that so few are willing in daily life to testify that Jesus is Lord.

What a call to prayer! Lord, teach Your disciples the blessedness of knowing Jesus and the power of His love; may they find their highest joy in witnessing to who He is and what He has done for them.

Day 11

The Gospel Ministry

"The Spirit of truth . . . will testify of Me. And you also will bear witness, because you have been with Me from the beginning." (John 15:26–27)

CHRIST'S call to bear witness refers to all believers, but it especially applies to ministers of the gospel. This is the high calling of the preacher of the gospel — and his only true power. This leads to two great truths.

The first is that, whatever Scripture passage the preacher teaches from and whatever may be the need of his congregation, he must first of all preach Christ Himself. This is what the early disciples did: "They did not cease teaching and preaching Jesus as the Christ" (Acts 5:42). This was what Philip did at Samaria: "Philip . . . preached Christ to them" (Acts 8:5). It is why Paul writes, "I determined not to know anything among you except Jesus Christ and Him crucified" (1 Cor. 2:2).

The minister of the gospel must never forget that he has been set apart specifically to be a witness for Christ through the Holy Spirit. As he does this, sinners will find salvation and God's children will be sanctified and fitted for His service. This is the only way Christ can have His place in the hearts of His people and in the world.

The second truth, which is no less important, is that the preacher's teaching must always be a personal testimony of what Christ is and can do. As the preacher speaks from his experience, the Holy Spirit carries the message as a living reality to the heart. This builds up believers so that they can walk in such fellowship with Jesus Christ that He can reveal Himself through them. And it leads them to the indispensable secret of spiritual health: a daily prayer life. This in turn cultivates among believers the joy of the Holy Spirit, in which, out of the abundance of the heart, the mouth speaks to the praise and glory of our blessed Redeemer, Jesus Christ our Lord.

Day 12

The Whole World

"You shall be witnesses to Me . . . to the ends of the earth." *(Acts 1:8)*

CHRIST said that His Church must aim for the whole world. But what kind of statement is this from a man who, in absolute impotence, had been crucified by His enemies? How dare He speak of the ends of the earth as His dominion!

This shows how foolish it is to speak of Christ as being nothing but a man. How could it have entered the mind of any writer to predict that a Jew who had been crucified, whose whole life was proven by that cross to be an utter failure, would conquer the world through His disciples — the same men who had utterly forsaken Him at His death? No human mind could have formed such a conception. It is the thought of God; He alone could plan and execute such a purpose.

The word Jesus spoke to His disciples — "You shall receive power when the Holy Spirit has come upon you" (Acts 1:8) — gave them the assurance that the Holy Spirit would maintain in them Christ's divine power. As Christ did His works only because the Father worked in Him, so Christ assured His disciples that He Himself from the throne of heaven would work all their works in them. They could ask for whatever they wanted and it would be done for them. In the strength of that promise the Church of Christ can make the ends of the earth its one aim.

The extension of God's kingdom can only be brought about by the united, continued prayer of men and women who give their hearts wholly to wait upon Christ, in the assurance that what they desire He will do for them.

May God grant that His children will prove their faith in Christ by making His aim their aim, and that they yield themselves to be His witnesses in united, persevering prayer. May they wait on Him in full assurance that He will surely and graciously give them all that they ask.

I challenge you to become one of those intercessors who really believe that in answer to your prayer the crucified Jesus will do far more than you can ask or think.

Day 13

The Whole Earth Filled with His Glory

And blessed be His glorious name forever!
And let the whole earth be filled with His glory. Amen and Amen.
(Psalm 72:19)

THINK of it — someday the earth, now under the power of the Evil One, will be renewed and filled with the glory of God — a new earth in which righteousness dwells! Though we may find it hard to believe, it will surely come to pass; God's Word is the pledge of it. God's Son conquered the power of sin by His death, and through the Eternal Spirit the power of God is working out His purpose. What a vision — the whole earth filled with His glory!

But what a mammoth and difficult work. Two thousand years after Christ gave the promise and ascended the throne, more than half of the human race have yet to hear the name of Jesus. And of the other half, millions who are called by His name do not know Him. The great work of bringing the knowledge of Christ to every creature has been entrusted to a Church that thinks little of her responsibility and of the consequences of her neglect. Will the work ever be done? His power and His faithfulness are pledges that one day we will see the whole earth filled with the glory of God. Blessed be His name!

The verse in Psalm 72 is a prayer: "Let the whole earth be filled with His glory. Amen and Amen." To this end every believer is called, and can count on the Holy Spirit to inspire and strengthen him. To this end we desire to strengthen each other, so that every day, with all our power, we may pray continually with one accord in faith, in the name of Jesus, and the power of His Spirit.

It is a blessing to know that true prayer will help — and will be answered! It is a blessing to seek God's face every day, to lay hold of Him with confidence and give Him no rest till the earth is full of His glory! Finally, it is a blessing to unite with all God's willing children in this day of His power — with all who are seeking to prepare the way for our King!

Day 14

The First Prayer Meeting

These all continued with one accord in prayer and supplication,
with the women and Mary . . . and with His brothers. (Acts 1:14)

THE early Church waited for the promise of the Father in united, unceasing prayer. It is difficult to form a right conception of the unspeakable importance of this first prayer meeting in the history of the kingdom, a meeting which was the result of simply fulfilling the command of Christ. It became for all time the indicator of the one condition through which His presence and Spirit would be known in power. In it we have the secret key that opens the storehouse of heaven with all its blessings.

Christ prayed that the disciples might be one, even as He and the Father were one, so that the world might know that God loved them as He loved Christ. How far the disciples were from that ideal at the time Christ prayed for them is seen in their argument at the Last Supper over who was the greatest (Luke 22:24). It was only after Christ had gone to heaven and they spent ten days in united supplication that they were brought to that holy unity of love and purpose which would make them the one Body of Christ, prepared to receive the Spirit in all His power.

What a prayer meeting! It was the fruit of Christ's training during His three years' companionship with them. Just as Adam's body was fully formed before God breathed the breath of life into him, the Body of Christ had to be formed before the Spirit took possession.

This prayer meeting gives us the law of the kingdom for all time. Wherever Christ's disciples are linked to each other in love and yield themselves wholly to Him in undivided consecration, the Spirit will be given from heaven as the seal of God's approval and Christ will show His mighty power. One of the great marks of the New Covenant is the united, unceasing prayer that avails much and is crowned with the power of the Holy Spirit.

If our prayers are not answered in the power that we hoped for, could the reason be that they are confined in great measure to our own church and our own interests?

Day 15

The Unity of the Spirit

Endeavoring to keep the unity of the Spirit. . . .
There is one body and one Spirit. (Eph. 4:3–4)

FROM Paul we learn how the Christian communities in different places ought to remember each other in the fellowship of prayer. He points out how in such prayer God is glorified. So he writes more than once (2 Cor. 1:11, 4:15, 9:12–13) of how the ministry of intercession abounds to the glory of God.

There is a great need today for the children of God throughout the world to draw close together, knowing that they are chosen by God to be a holy priesthood, ministering continually the sacrifice of praise and prayer. There is too little distinction between the world and the Body of Christ; the lives of many of God's children are not much different from the world. What can be done to foster the unity of the Spirit?

The biggest step is for believers to commit to a life of more prayer, specifically interceding that God's people may prove their unity in a life of holiness and love. That will be a living testimony to the world of what it means to live for God. When Paul wrote, "Praying always with all prayer and supplication in the Spirit, being watchful to this end with all perseverance and supplication for all the saints" (Eph. 6:18), he named one of the essential characteristics of the difference between God's people and the world.

Do you long to bear this mark of the children of God? Do you desire to be able to pray for the saints in a way that proves to yourself and others that you are not of the world? Resolve in your heart to put into practice this one great distinctive feature of the true Christian life. Join with God's children who are seeking with one accord to maintain the unity of the Spirit. Join with them to pray down a blessing upon His Church.

Is it too much to give fifteen minutes a day to meditation on a Scripture passage connected with His promises to His Church — and then plead with Him for its fulfillment? If you do, slowly but surely you will taste the blessedness of being one with God's people and receive the power to pray the effective, fervent prayer that avails much (James 5:16).

Day 16

Union Is Strength

And when they had prayed . . . they were all filled with the Holy Spirit, and they spoke the word of God with boldness. Now the multitude of those who believed were of one heart and one soul. (Acts 4:31–32)

THE power of union is seen everywhere in nature. How feeble is a drop of rain as it falls to earth. But when many drops are united in one stream, becoming one body, soon their power is irresistible. Such is the power of true union in prayer. The marginal reading of Psalm 34:5 is, instead of "They looked to Him," "They flowed to Him." The Dutch translation is, "They rushed towards Him like a stream of water." Such was the prayer in the upper room. And such can our prayer be if we unite all our forces in pleading the promise of the Father. And when the world "comes in like a flood," it can be overcome in the power of united prayer.

In Natal, owing to the many mountains, the streams often flow down with great force. When the Zulus cross a stream, they join hands. The leader has a strong stick in his right hand and gives his left hand to some strong man who comes behind him. And so they form a chain of twelve or twenty, and help each other to cross the current. When God's people reach out their hands to each other, there is power to resist the terrible influence that the world can exert. And in that unity God's children, when they have overcome the power of the world and the flesh, will have power to prevail with God.

The disciples stayed in the upper room for ten days until they had truly become one heart and one soul. When the Spirit of God descended, He not only filled each individual but took possession of the whole company as the Body of Christ.

Our Lord Jesus is still praying, "Father, that they may be one as We are one." In the fellowship of loving and believing prayer, our hearts can be melted into one and we will become strong in faith to believe and accept what God has promised us.

Day 17

Prayer in the Name of Christ

"And whatever you ask in My name, that will I do,
that the Father may be glorified in the Son." (John 14:13)

THE link between our prayers and Christ's glorifying the Father in heaven is wonderful. Abundant prayer on earth brings Him abundant glory in heaven. Little prayer means, as far as we are concerned, little glory to the Father. What an incentive to prayer, to unceasing intercession! Our prayer is indispensable to the glorifying of the Father.

So deep was the desire of Christ to teach His disciples to believe in the power of His name that we find His promise of answered prayer repeated seven times on the night He was betrayed. He knew how slow men are to believe.

He longs to stir up in us a large and confident faith, to free our prayers from every shadow of doubt, and to teach us to look on intercession as the most certain and most blessed way of bringing glory to God, joy to our own souls, and blessing to the perishing world around us.

And if we think we cannot attain such a level of prayer, we only need to remember what Christ told them — that when the Holy Spirit came they would have the power to pray. To encourage us to yield ourselves fully to the Spirit's control, He holds out to us this precious promise: "Ask, and you will receive, that your joy may be full" (John 16:24). As we believe in the power of the Spirit working in us fully, intercession will become the joy and strength of all our service.

When Paul wrote, "Whatever you do in word or deed, do all in the name of the Lord Jesus" (Col. 3:17), he reminds us how in daily life everything is to bear the signature of Jesus. As we learn to do this — as we live in that name before men — we can come to the Father with the full confidence that our prayer in that name will be answered. Our life in fellowship with men is to be one with our life in communion with God. When the name of Jesus rules all in our life, it will give power to our prayers also.

Day 18

Your Heavenly Father

"Our Father in heaven . . ." (Matt. 6:9)

HOW simple and beautiful is this invocation which Christ puts on our lips! And yet how inconceivably rich it is in its meaning, in the fullness of the love and blessing it contains.

Volumes could be written about wise and loving earthly fathers. This world owes so much to fathers who have made their children strong and happy by giving their lives to seek the welfare of their fellow men. But all this is just a shadow — a shadow of exquisite beauty, yet only a shadow — of what the Father in heaven is to His children on earth.

What a gift Christ bestowed on us when He gave us the right to say, "Our Father."

And He is "our Father in heaven," our heavenly Father. We count it a great privilege as we bow in worship to know that the Father comes near to us where we are on earth. But we also sense the need to rise up and enter into His holy presence in heaven, to breathe its atmosphere, to drink in its spirit, and to become truly heavenly-minded. And as we in the power of thought and imagination leave earth behind, and in the power of the Holy Spirit enter the Holiest of All, where the seraphs worship, the term "heavenly Father" takes on a new meaning, and our hearts come under an influence that we can walk in all day long.

Christ reminded His listeners about the love of earthly fathers, and then added, "How much more will your heavenly Father give the Holy Spirit to those who ask Him!" (Luke 11:13). When Christ says, "How much more," we feel the distance between the earthly picture and the heavenly reality, and can only bow in lowly, loving adoration, saying, "Father, our Father, my Father."

May God give us grace to cultivate a heavenly spirit, proving every day that we are children of our Father in heaven, and love to dwell in His holy presence!

Day 19

The Power of Prayer

The effective, fervent prayer of a righteous man avails much. (James 5:16)

PRAYER avails much. It avails much with God. It avails much in the history of His Church and people. Prayer is the one great power which the Church can exercise to unleash God's omnipotence in the world.

The prayer of a righteous man avails much. This is speaking of a man who has the righteousness of Christ not only as a garment covering him but as a life-power inspiring him, as a new man "created in righteousness and true holiness" (Eph. 4:24). He is a man who lives as a "servant to righteousness" (Rom. 6:16, 19), whom the Lord loves and whose prayer has power (Ps. 66:18–19; 1 John 3:22). When Christ gave His great prayer promises at the Last Supper, it was to those who kept His commandments: "If you love Me, keep My commandments. And I will pray the Father, and He will give you another Helper" (John 14:15–16). "If you keep My commandments, you will abide in My love" (John 15:10); "If you abide in Me . . . you will ask what you desire, and it shall be done for you" (15:7).

It is also a fervent prayer. It is only when the righteous man stirs up his whole being to take hold of God that the prayer avails much. Just as Jacob said, "I will not let You go until You bless me" (Gen. 32:26), and as the persistent widow gave the unjust judge no rest (Luke 18:1–5), so the effective, fervent prayer brings about great things.

Then there is the effective, fervent prayer of *many* righteous. When two or three agree, there is the promise of an answer. How much more when hundreds and thousands unite with one accord to cry to God to display His mighty power on behalf of His people.

Let us join those who have united themselves to call upon God for the mighty power of the Holy Spirit in His Church. What a great and blessed work this is, and how confident we can be, in God's time, of an abundant answer! Let us pray to God, individually and unitedly, for the grace of the effective, fervent prayer which avails much.

Day 20

Prayer and Sacrifice

For I want you to know what a great conflict I have for you. (Col. 2:1)

THOSE who undertake great exploits must prepare themselves, summoning all their powers to their aid. Christians need to prepare themselves to pray "with their whole heart and strength." This is the law of the kingdom. Prayer requires sacrifice of ease, of time, of self. The secret to powerful prayer is sacrifice.

This was true of Christ Jesus, the great Intercessor. It is written of Him, "When You make His soul an offering for sin, He shall see His seed. . . . He shall divide the spoil with the strong, because He poured out His soul unto death" (Isa. 53:10, 12). In Gethsemane "He . . . offered up prayers and supplications, with vehement cries and tears" (Heb. 5:7). Prayer is sacrifice. David said, "Let my prayer be set forth before You as incense, the lifting up of my hands as the evening sacrifice" (Ps. 141:2).

Prayer is based on sacrifice. Our prayer is only worthy because it is rooted in the sacrifice of Jesus Christ. As He gave up everything in His prayer "Thy will be done," our attitude must always be to offer up of everything to God and His service.

A pious Welsh miner had a relative whom the doctor ordered to Madeira for recuperation. But there was no money. The miner resolved to take the little money that he had and use it all. He procured comfortable lodgings for the invalid, but was content with a small room for himself, and lived on a tight budget. He spent much time in prayer until he got the assurance that the invalid would recover. On the last day of the month the sick one was well. When the miner reached home, he said that he had now learned more than ever that the secret law and the hidden power of prayer lay in self-sacrifice.

Need we wonder at the lack of power in our prayers when we are so reluctant to sacrifice ourselves in waiting on God? Christ, the Christ we trust in, the Christ who lives in us, offered Himself as a sacrifice to God. As this spirit lives and rules in us, we will receive power from Him as intercessors to pray the effective prayer that avails much.

Day 21

The Intercession of the Spirit for the Saints

Now he who searches the hearts knows what the mind of the Spirit is, because He makes intercession for the saints according to the will of God. (Rom. 8:27)

WHAT light these words shed on the life of prayer in the hearts of the saints! Paul says that "we do not know what we should pray for as we ought," which hinders our prayer — or hinders the faith that is essential to its success. But he adds, for our encouragement, that "the Spirit Himself makes intercession for us with groanings which cannot be uttered" (Rom. 8:26).

Where and how does the Spirit make intercession for the saints? In the heart which knows not what to pray, He secretly and effectively prays what is according to the will of God. This, of course, implies that we trust Him to do His work in us, and that we wait before God even when we do not know what to pray, in the assurance that the Holy Spirit is praying in us. This implies further that we take time to wait in God's presence, that we exercise an unbounded dependence on the Holy Spirit who has been given us to cry "Abba, Father" within us, even when we have nothing to offer but groanings and sighs which cannot be verbalized.

What a difference it would make in the life of many of God's saints if they realized this! Not only do we have Jesus the Son of God, the great High Priest, always interceding for us; not only do we have the liberty to ask in faith for what we desire and the promise that it shall be given us; but we have the Holy Spirit, "the Spirit of grace and supplication," carrying on, in the depths of our being, His work of interceding for each of us according to the will of God.

What a call to separate ourselves from the world, to yield ourselves whole-heartedly to the leading and praying of the Spirit within us, deeper than all our thoughts or expectations! What a call to surrender ourselves in stillness of soul, resting in the Lord and waiting patiently for Him, as the Holy Spirit prays within us not only for ourselves but for all saints, according to the will of God!

Day 22

That They All May Be One

"Holy Father, keep through Your name those whom You have given Me, that they may be one as We are. . . . I do not pray for these alone, but also for those who will believe in Me through their word; that they all may be one, as You, Father, are in Me, and I in you; that they also may be one in Us. . . . And the glory which You gave Me I have given them, that they may be one just as We are one: I in them, and You in Me; that they may be made perfect in one; and that the world may know that You have sent Me." (John 17:11, 20–23)

NOTICE carefully how the Lord uses the expression "that they may be one" five times over. It is as if He felt a need to lay the emphasis strongly on these words if we are truly to realize the chief thought of His High Priestly prayer. He longs for these words to have the same place in our hearts that they have in His.

As He was on the way to go to the Father through the cross, He wanted us to understand that He took this desire with Him to heaven, to make it the object of His unceasing intercession there. And He entrusted the words to us that we should take them into the world with us and make them the object of our unceasing intercession. That alone would enable us to fulfill the new command He gave, to love the brethren as He loved us, so that our joy might be full.

How little the Church has understood this. How little are its different branches marked by a fervent, affectionate love to all the saints of whatever name or denomination. Why not make this prayer "that they may be one" a chief part of your daily fellowship with God?

How simple it is to connect the two words "Our Father" with all the children of God throughout the world. Each time we use these sacred words, we only have to expand this little word "Our" into all the largeness and richness of God's Father-love. As naturally as we say "Father" with the thought of His infinite love and of our love for Him, we can say "Our" with childlike affection for all the saints of God, whoever and wherever they may be. The prayer "that they may be one" would then become a joy and a strength, a deeper bond of fellowship with Christ Jesus and all His saints, and an offering with a sweet savor to the Father of love.

Day 23

The Disciples' Prayer

These all continued with one accord in prayer and supplication. . . . And they continued steadfastly in the apostles' doctrine and fellowship, in the breaking of bread, and in prayers. (Acts 1:14, 2:42)

WE can learn a lot from a clear picture of what this "continuing with one accord in prayer" meant to the disciples.

The object of their desire was the Comforter whom Jesus had promised. No matter how defective their concept was of the Blessed Spirit, they certainly knew, from the words of Jesus, that "It is to your advantage that I go away" (John 16:7). They also knew that the Spirit would place the glorified Christ in their hearts in a way they had never known before. And it would be He Himself, in the mighty power of God's Spirit, who would be their strength for the work to which He had called them.

With what confidence they expected the fulfillment of the promise! Had not the Master, who loved them so well, given them the assurance of what He would send to them from the throne of the Father in heaven?

In the midst of the praise and thanksgiving that filled their hearts as they worshiped their Lord in heaven, they prayed, remembering all He had taught them about persistence in prayer, in full assurance that however long the answer might be delayed, He would most assuredly fulfill their desires. Let us nourish our hearts with thoughts such as these, until we realize that the very same promise that was given to the disciples is given to us, and that we too, even though we have to cry day and night to God, can count upon the Father to answer our prayers.

And last but not least, just as they continued with one accord in prayer, we can unite as one in presenting our petitions, even though we cannot be together in one place. In the love through which His Spirit makes us one, and in the experience of our Lord's presence with each one of us, we can claim the promise that we, too, shall be filled with the Holy Spirit.

Day 24

Paul's Call to Prayer

*Praying always with all prayer and supplication in the Spirit, being watchful
to this end with all perseverance and supplication for all the saints.
(Eph. 6:18–19)*

WHAT a sense Paul had of the deep, divine unity of the whole Body of
Christ and the need for unceasing prayer for all the members of the Body.
He did not mean this to be an occasional thing, but an unceasing exercise of
their life together. This is evident from the words he uses: "With all prayer and
supplication in the Spirit, being watchful to this end with all perseverance and
supplication for all the saints." He expects believers to be so conscious of being
in Christ, and through Him united to the whole Body, that in their daily life
their highest aim would always be the welfare of the Body. He assumes they are
filled with the Spirit, so that it is perfectly natural to them, and never a burden,
to pray for all who belong to the Body of Christ. It is as natural as it is for each
member of a physical body to do what contributes to the welfare of the whole.
Being united with Christ also means I am united in joy and love with all the
members of His Body.

Isn't this just what we need in our daily life? Every believer who has yielded
himself completely to Christ Jesus should daily live in the consciousness that he
is one with Christ and His body. Just as a time of war reveals the willingness of the
citizens to sacrifice for their country, so the saints of God should be willing to
offer a sacrifice of prayer and intercession at all times and for all saints!

Day 25

Paul's Request for Prayer

And for me, that utterance may be given to me, that I may open my mouth boldly
to make known the mystery of the gospel . . . that in it I may speak boldly,
as I ought to speak. (Eph. 6:19–20)

PAUL'S request for himself shows the depth of his faith in the absolute necessity and wonderful power of prayer. And it is significant that he asks them to pray "that . . . I may speak boldly, as I ought to speak."

Paul had been a minister of the gospel for more than twenty years when he wrote this. One would assume that by now it would come naturally to him to "speak boldly." But he was so deeply convinced of his own insufficiency and weakness, and his absolute dependence on divine teaching and power, that he felt that without the direct help of God he could not do the work as it ought to be done. The sense of his total and unalterable dependence upon God, who was with him, teaching him what and how to speak, is the basis of all his confidence and the keynote of his whole life.

But there is more. Countless times during these twenty years he had been in circumstances where he had to throw himself upon God alone, with no one to help him in prayer. And yet, so deep is his spiritual insight into the unity of the Body of Christ and his dependence on the prayers of others, that he pleads for them to pray for him "with all prayer and supplication in the Spirit, being watchful to this end with all perseverance" (Eph. 6:18–19). Just as a wrestler cannot do without the help of even the weakest member of his body in the struggle in which he is engaged, Paul could not do without the prayers of the believers.

This is a call to us today to awake to the consciousness that Christ, our Intercessor in heaven, and all saints here upon earth, are engaged in a mighty battle. Our duty is to cultivate the gift of unceasing supplication — to pray for the power of God's Spirit in all His servants, that divine utterance may be given to them, so that they may speak boldly and as they ought to speak.

Day 26

Prayer for All Saints

We give thanks to the God and Father of our Lord Jesus Christ, praying always for
you, since we heard of your faith in Christ Jesus and of your love for all the saints. . . .
Continue earnestly in prayer, being vigilant in it with thanksgiving;
meanwhile praying also for us. (Col. 1:3–4, 4:2–3)

MAY our first thought be to pray "for all the saints." It takes time, and thought, and love, to realize what that simple expression involves. Think of your own community and the saints you know; think of your country, and praise God for all who are His saints; think of the Christian nations of the world, and the saints to be found in each of these; think of all the non-Christian nations and the saints of God to be found among them in ever-increasing numbers.

Think of all the different circumstances and conditions in which these are to be found and all the greatly varying needs which call for God's grace and help. Think of many who are God's saints, and yet through ignorance or sloth, through worldly-mindedness or an evil heart of unbelief, are walking in the dark and bringing no honor to God. Think of so many who are in earnest and yet conscious of a life of failure, with little or no power to please God or to bless man. And then think again of those who are to be found everywhere, in solitary places or in companies, whose one aim is to serve the Lord who bought them. Think of them, often unconscious of their relation to the whole Body of Christ, joining in pleading for the great promise of the Holy Spirit and the love and oneness of heart which He alone can give.

This is not the work of one day or one night. It requires a heart which will set itself from time to time to do serious thinking in regard to the state and the needs of the Body of Christ to which we belong. But when once we begin, we shall find what abundant reason there is for our persevering and yielding to God's Spirit, so that He may fit us for the great and blessed work of day by day praying a twofold prayer: for the love of God and Christ to fill the hearts of His people, and for the power of the Holy Spirit to come down and accomplish God's work in this sinful world.

Day 27

Prayer by All Saints

We trust in God that He will still deliver us . . . you also helping together in prayer for us. (2 Cor. 1:10–11)

For I know that this will turn out for my salvation, through your prayer and the supply of the Spirit of Jesus Christ. (Phil. 1:19)

THESE verses call us once again to think of all saints throughout the world but lead us to view them from a different standpoint. When we ask God to increase the number and the power of those who pray, what are we really asking for? What will it look like to see the circle of intercessors gradually increase in number and power?

The first thing we may naturally think of is the many believers who have very little interest in pleading in prayer for the strengthening of the Body of Christ. We need to remind ourselves that there are also many — and we praise God for them — who do intercede for the power of God's Spirit to rest on His people. Sadly, however, the prayers of these loyal intercessors are often limited to spheres of work that they are acquainted with or directly interested in.

That leaves us with what is, comparatively speaking, the very small number of those who are ready to take part in the kind of prayer which ought to be sent up by the whole Church — prayer for the unity of the Body and the power of the Spirit. And even then the number may be even smaller who really feel drawn to take part in daily prayer for the outpouring of the Spirit on all God's people.

And yet many may feel that making Christ's last prayer, "that they may be one," into a daily supplication, meets a long-felt need, and is an unspeakable privilege, whether they join in with few or many. It may be that in time believers will band together in small circles, or in wider gatherings, to help rouse those around them to take part in the great work, that the prayer for all the saints may be prayed by all the saints.

This message is written to all who will listen, with the hope of increasing their commitment to pray daily for the power of His love and Spirit to be revealed to all His people.

Day 28

Prayer for All the Fullness of the Spirit

"Bring all the tithes into the storehouse, . . . and prove Me now in this," says the Lord of hosts, "If I will not open for you the windows of heaven and pour out for you such blessing that there will not be room enough to receive it." (Mal. 3:10)

THIS last promise in the Old Testament tells us how abundant the blessing is to be — beyond our capacity to receive it! Pentecost was only the beginning of what God was willing to do. The promise of the Father, as Christ gave it, still waits for its complete fulfillment. Do we realize what liberty we have to ask and expect great things?

Just as Christ's great command to go and preach the gospel was not only meant for the disciples but for us too, so His very last command, "Tarry . . . until you are endued with power from on high" (Luke 24:49) is also for us. It is the ground for our confident assurance that our prayer with one accord will be heard.

Imagine the many needs throughout the whole Church and in the mission fields across the globe. The only remedy for spiritual ineffectiveness and impotence, the only way to gain victory over the powers of darkness, is in the manifested presence of our Lord in the midst of His hosts and in the power of His Spirit.

Think of the spiritual condition of the various churches throughout the world. It should convince you more thoroughly than ever that nothing can succeed except the supernatural, almighty intervention of our Lord Himself. He must rouse His hosts for the great battle against evil. Is there any other matter for prayer that can compete with this? Pray for the power of God on the ministers of the gospel, and on all His people, to endue them with power from on high to make the gospel in very deed the power of God unto salvation.

As we connect prayer for the whole Church on earth with prayer for the whole power of God in heaven, we will feel that the greatest truths of the heavenly world and the kingdom of God have possession of us, and that we are asking what God is longing to give, as soon as He finds hearts utterly yielded to Him in faith and obedience.

Day 29

Every Day

"Give us day by day our daily bread." (Luke 11:3)

SOME Christians are afraid of making a promise to pray for others every day. Such a commitment seems beyond their power. And yet they pray to God to give them their bread day by day. But a child of God who has yielded his whole life to God's love and service should consider it a privilege to make a promise that gives him the chance to come into God's presence every day with the needs of His Church and kingdom.

Many believers claim that they desire to live wholly for God. They acknowledge that Christ gave Himself for them and continues to work in them. They agree that nothing less than Christ's love for us is the standard by which we measure our love for Him. Surely they ought to welcome any opportunity to prove that they are devoting their heart's strength to the interests of Christ's kingdom, and to the kind of prayer that brings down God's blessing.

An invitation to daily united prayer may be to you a new and unexpected opportunity to cry to God day and night for His power and blessing on His people and on this needy world. Think of the privilege of being allowed to plead with God on behalf of His saints for the outpouring of His Spirit, for the coming of His kingdom, for His will to be done on earth as it is in heaven.

Those who have never fully understood what a great privilege and duty it is to wait on God in prayer for His blessing on the world should welcome this invitation to pray. Even those who already pray daily for a particular ministry or group may be encouraged to enlarge their vision, as well as their hearts, to include all God's saints, all the work of His kingdom, and all the promise of an abundant outpouring of His Spirit. Taking part in this ministry of prayer for the whole Church should not cause their prayer for their particular group to suffer; instead, their hearts will be strengthened with a joy, a love and a faith that they have never known before.

Day 30

With One Accord

They were all with one accord in one place. . . .
And they were all filled with the Holy Spirit. (Acts 2:1, 4)

THE subject of united prayer reveals the solidarity of the whole Body of Christ and shows the need for deliberate cultivation of the slumbering talents of intercession. We should thank God for the tens of thousands of His children who pray daily for some portion of the work of God's kingdom. But if their prayers are limited to the work they take an interest in, they lack that large-hearted and universal love that embraces all the saints of God and their service. They do not have the boldness and the strength that comes from being part of a large, victorious army under the leadership of our conquering King.

In a time of war, each unit of soldiers throws its whole heart into the work that it has to do. But it also rejoices and takes new courage from every report of the bravery and enthusiasm of the far-distant members of the one great army.

Isn't this what we need in the Church of Christ — an enthusiasm for the King and His kingdom, and faith in His purpose that His name shall be made known to every human being? Then our prayers will rise up every day with a large-hearted love that grasps the whole Body of Christ and pleads daily for the power of the Holy Spirit on all its members, even the very feeblest.

The strength that unity gives is something inconceivable. The power of each individual member is greatly increased by the inspiring fellowship of a large and conquering host. Nothing can so help us to an ever-larger faith as the consciousness of being one body and one spirit in Christ Jesus. It was as the disciples were all with one accord in one place on the Day of Pentecost that they were all filled with the Holy Spirit. United prayer brings the answer to prayer!

Day 31

A Personal Call

We should not trust in ourselves but in God who raises the dead, who delivered us.
(2 Cor. 1:9–10)

For I know that this will turn out for my salvation through your prayer and
the supply of the Spirit of Jesus Christ. (Phil. 1:19)

PAUL'S comment to the Philippians proves that there were still Spirit-filled Christians in the churches whom Paul could count on for effective, much-availing prayer — despite the lukewarmness of many others.

When we plead with Christians to pray without ceasing, a large number quietly decide that such a life is not possible for them. They do not have any special gift for prayer, or any intense desire to glorify Christ in the salvation of souls; they have yet to learn how the power of the constraining love of Christ can enable them to live not for themselves but for Him who died for them and rose again.

If you fall into this category, I want to call on you to offer yourself in wholehearted surrender to live entirely for Christ. Are you not ashamed of the selfish life that simply uses Christ as a convenience to escape from hell and to secure a place in heaven? I can assure you that God can change your life and fill your heart with Christ and His Holy Spirit. I plead with you to believe that with God all things are possible. He is able and willing, even anxious, to restore you to the Father's house, to the joy of His presence and service.

One step on the way to attaining this is to listen to the call for men and women who will, every day and all the day, in the power of Christ's abiding presence, live in the spirit of unceasing intercession for all saints. Receive the power of the Holy Spirit, and acknowledge that this is nothing less than a duty, a sacrifice that Christ's love has a right to claim, and that He by His Spirit will indeed work in you.

Any believer, however far he may have come short, who accepts the call as coming from Christ and draws near to God in humble prayer for the needed grace, will have taken the first step on the path that leads to fellowship with God, to a new faith and life in Christ Jesus, and to the surrender of his whole being to that intercession of the Spirit that will help to bring Pentecost again into the hearts of God's people.

PUBLICATIONS

Fort Washington, PA 19034

This book is published by CLC Publications, an outreach of CLC Ministries International. The purpose of CLC is to make evangelical Christian literature available to all nations so that people may come to faith and maturity in the Lord Jesus Christ. We hope this book has been life changing and has enriched your walk with God through the work of the Holy Spirit. If you would like to know more about CLC, we invite you to visit our website:

www.clcusa.org

To know more about the remarkable story of the founding of CLC International we encourage you to read

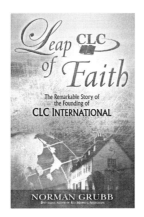

LEAP OF FAITH

Norman Grubb

Paperback
Size 5¹/₄ x 8, Pages 248
ISBN: 978-0-87508-650-7
ISBN (e-book): 978-1-61958-055-8